Intentionally Inclusive

Together at the Table for Ministry

Marcia J. Patton

Edited by Kathryn V. Stanley

Foreword by Eric H. F. Law

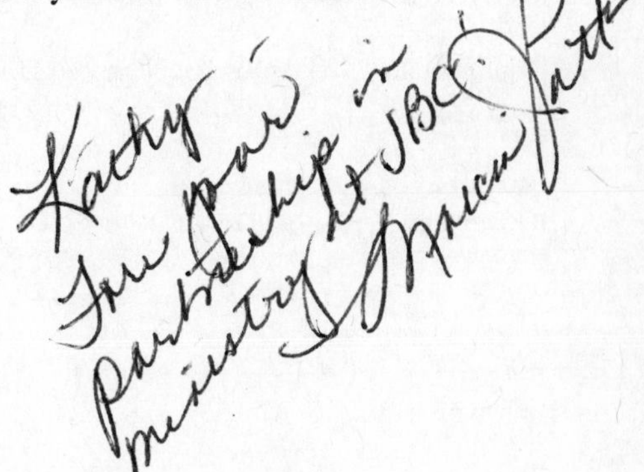

Intentionally Inclusive: Together at the Table for Ministry

Judson Press has made every effort to trace the ownership of all quotes. In the event of a question arising from the use of a quote, we regret any error made and will be pleased to make the necessary correction in future printings and editions of this book.

The Voices of Evergreen are adapted from the Evergreen newsletter found at www.evergreen-abc.org/newsarchive/html.

Interior design by Wendy Ronga/Hampton Design Group.
Cover design by Lisa Delgado/Delgado and Company, Inc.

Library of Congress Cataloging-in-Publication data
Cataloging-in-Publication Data available upon request.
Contact cip@judsonpress.com.

Printed in the U.S.A.

First printing, 2017.

Dedicated to two American Baptists
who worked diligently toward
the inclusion of all people:

Rev. Dr. Paul Nagano,
from the pulpit and through
the church and its agencies.

The Honorable Charles Z. Smith,
from the bench of the Washington Supreme Court
and in the classroom teaching law and ethics.

They planted the seed; others watered.
God's work continues to grow.

Contents

Foreword by Eric H. F. Law vi
Preface ix
Acknowledgments xiii
Introduction xv

1. Getting the Table Ready 1
2. Culture and Communications at the Table 17
3. Consensus 34
4. Cultural Sensitivity 52
5. It's All about Relationships 62

Excursus: How Did It All Begin 85
Epilogue 99

APPENDICES
A. Bylaws of the Evergreen Association of American Baptist Churches 102
B. American Baptist Churches USA Identity Statement 1998 116
C. ABCUSA Code of Ethics for Ministerial Leaders 121

Notes 124

Foreword

I have been telling the Evergreen story in my teaching and consulting ministry ever since I met Marcia Patton in 2006. As I recalled, she had read some of my books, including *The Wolf Shall Dwell with the Lamb,* and decided to come and check out the summer training program that the Kaleidoscope Institute provided that year. Since then, we have stayed in touch. Throughout the continuing development and formation of Evergreen, sometimes, I acted as a coach to her as she discerned what her next move might be or how to handle a difficult situation. Other times, I was invited to do additional leadership training for the good people at Evergreen. I was and still am grateful that Marcia decided to include the resources that I have developed over the years to nurture and develop the Evergreen Association as an intentionally inclusive organization.

Talking about being multicultural is different from being an inclusive community. Anyone who has attempted to build a truly inclusive community knows that it required intentionality. Without intentional facilitation of relationship-building and truth-telling, we generally revert back to old patterns of behavior that are not inclusive. One of these patterns is what I have called "the wolf-and-lamb scenario," in which one group dominates the proceeding, while other individuals or groups seem to "let them." The dominant group does the talking while the others are silent. Even when there is a great effort in bringing people from diverse backgrounds together physically in one room, this scenario takes over and the silent ones will leave and usually do not come back for future gatherings. Traditional styles of running a meeting in European

American culture, such as Robert's Rules of Order, do not seem to help this wolf-and-lamb dynamic, even though such a model makes the claim, "The application of parliamentary law is the best method yet devised to enable assemblies of any size, with due regard for every member's opinion, to arrive at the general will on the maximum number of questions of varying complexity in a minimum amount of time...."[1]

Organizations often harbor a misconception that if we think it, want it, believe it, or say that we should be an inclusive community, it will happen. Marcia did not just think it, want it, and believe it; with perseverance of consistent actions, she empowered the people of Evergreen to live the sometimes uneasy way of being an inclusive community. These acts of inclusion include creation of organizational structure such as the caucuses and effective use of tools and processes such as the Respectful Communication Guidelines, Mutual Invitation, and consensus decision-making. And the result is amazing, as shown through the many witnesses who share their parts in the story of Evergreen in this book.

This book is not just for American Baptists, who are family to the Evergreen Association. This book is for anyone who wants to learn how to building an inclusive community. Read the Excursus first if you want to know how the American Baptist organization works. But before you decide that Evergreen's story is just an American Baptist thing, you must appreciate the struggles that Marcia and her colleagues faced every step of the way toward becoming the thriving inclusive community that it is today.

This book is an essential resource for those who have influence on an organizational level of any church body, local, regional, or national. The political challenges that church leaders face in other denominations might be different, but the struggle to be intentionally inclusive is the same. Marcia has put forth a template and process for developing an intentionally inclusive community at almost any level of faith-based organization. Read this book, reflect on it, and discuss it with leaders of your community. Experiment with the processes and tools contained herein, and envision how to transform your community from being multicultural to acting inclusively, from reacting out of fear to living into the abundant grace of God, and from holding on to old ways to embracing God's call to strive for justice and peace among all people and respect the dignity of every human being.

Rev. Dr. Eric H. F. Law
Founder and Executive Director
Kaleidoscope Institute

Note

1. *Robert's Rules of Order Newly Revised* [RONR (11th ed.), Introduction, p. liii]. http://www.rulesonline.com/

Preface

It was the late 1990s. The controversial presidential race between Bush and Gore was over; the evangelical church was immersed in the political scene; and the issue of LGBTQ rights had taken center stage politically as well as in the church. Then, as we entered a new century, the terrible horror of September 11 rocked the nation. It was against this backdrop that the story of the Evergreen Association emerged. As our story continued to unfold, America elected its first African American president, which set the country on a course that both helped undergird Evergreen's mission and made the work that we do much more important.

The Evergreen story takes place primarily in Seattle. On the Good Friday before September 11 an earthquake hit Seattle. It wasn't the worst earthquake the Seattle area had experienced, but it hit the downtown core and toppled steeples at Seattle First Baptist Church. The players in this story are American Baptist congregations in and around Seattle.

Another important player in this story is American Baptist Churches USA, one segment of a wider denomination that has been in America since the colonizers first came.

Dissenters in Massachusetts, the Baptists had to leave that colony if we wanted to practice our faith as we saw fit. We claim Roger Williams of Rhode Island as one of our American forebearers. He, along with other Baptists, worked to make sure that the Rhode Island charter included religious freedom. Roger Williams even gave some recompense to the Native Americans for the land he used. It was other Baptists who insisted that the Constitution would not be complete without the First Amendment, which guaranteed religious freedom.

One of the tenets of Baptist faith is the belief in "soul liberty," which says that you are responsible for *your* journey with God, as I am responsible for *my* journey with God. I can't tell you exactly how to come to God any more than you can tell me what my walk with God ought to be. It is out of this belief that Baptists pressed James Madison and others for the First Amendment. We were not the majority faith group in any colony, and we knew the injustice of taxation to support faith groups with which we didn't agree and the forced compliance with laws we felt were in opposition to our faith.

Another tenet of Baptist life and identity is the "Associational Principle." This principle is the belief that we should connect with one another as local communities of faith, that a life with other Baptist churches is better lived than life without collaboration with others. Unlike connectional churches that stem from "one church," Baptist churches do not have that notion of being one universal church. In fact, our denomination made sure of that by including plurality in our name: American Baptist *Churches* USA. We are autonomous local churches freely "associating" with one another. There is as much diversity of thought among Baptists about how to do the work as there are Baptist groups, which is why there are so many different groups.

Evergreen has been "revolutionary" even in Baptist traditions, such that others have taken note of our work. For example, the late Rev. Dr. James Dunn, past executive director of the Baptist Joint Committee, an advocacy group based in Washington DC that does primary work on First Amendment rights, wrote while teaching at Wake Forest Seminary: "I use Evergreen as my illustration of what a Baptist Association is and *ought to be*" (emphasis his). How amazing that a respected biblical scholar and theologian who knew many Baptist groups well used our organization as a prototype of the way Baptist associations ought to be!

I wish I could say that becoming what the Baptist associations "ought to be" was our intent. I wish I could say that in this book you will discover a step-by-step plan for becoming what we have become. But the truth is that Evergreen didn't evolve that way. We never consulted "Baptist experts," or even organizational or multicultural experts, on how to build an inclusive Baptist association. By the grace of God, fervent prayer, and the concerted efforts of many who desired to be open to others, Evergreen was born and continues to thrive.

The Baptist ideals of soul liberty, local church autonomy, and the principle of association combined with the West's fair amount of "pioneer thinking," as well as the ingredients for out-of-the-box thinking and acting, emerged to make Evergreen possible. We took these steps because of this background, these ideals, and the peculiarities of our context.

The context of this story also rests on the radical change of pastors happening in greater Seattle American Baptist congregations at the time. These changes in leadership created fertile ground for the organizational shifts Evergreen would make. These shifts occurred among African American, Asian American, and Euro American congregations in Seattle and Tacoma.

Against this backdrop and through the lens of the Evergreen experiment, this book traces the development of an inclusive organization. An inclusive ministry is what Evergreen Association of American Baptist Churches seeks to be and do. We didn't necessarily set out to do great work in this area; we were just trying to include all the congregations and people that were a part of American Baptist Churches USA in a particular geographical area.

This book contains a bit of intercultural theory, but only as it relates to the Evergreen story. Intercultural theory is beyond my expertise, and I do not want to disrespect the many fine scholars who have published elsewhere on that subject. While I will make some theological arguments for diversity, we didn't engage in theological discussions about our work. This is really a story of a group of Christian people trying their best to live out what we sense God calling us to do. Therefore, it would be disingenuous for me to write as though we had approached our work and ministry with deep theological reflection.

Ours is a story which needs telling—but not just for ourselves (though we like good stories), not even for the American Baptist Churches USA, and not just for the wider Baptist bodies, but for the world to know that a few folks in the western part of the United States are trying to put their Christian values to work as we work with one another. Too often, especially in Baptist circles, it doesn't even seem that individuals within one Baptist tradition can get along, let alone relate with civility and creativity with other Baptists or other Christians. We are aware that the world needs Christ's message of peace, goodwill, and unity more than anything these days. This narrative brings one of those good stories to you.

We have also come to believe that as the United States becomes more and more pluralistic, our experience of inclusion is needed in the wider world. We have all been stretched; we have all grown. Most of us still have a lot of stretching and growing to do, and we see many of our acquaintances and friends just starting down that path. Our hope is that this story will offer encouragement. If this small group can have a positive experience of including diverse people, so can the next group. We believe it is possible! It is our hope that our story will become your story.

Acknowledgments

So much goes into the writing of a book, especially one whose purpose is to tell a history. The whole Evergreen family deserves thanks; without the courage and faith that God was leading us, this story would not have happened. I must thank two people in particular without whom this book probably would not have been written: Yosh Nakagawa and Clem Winbush. Yosh, because at least every other conversation he reminded me that the "history of Evergreen" must be written and it must be written by us! "Don't let someone else tell our story, Marcia!" Clem, because without her support, I could not have taken the time to write, would have given much worse copy to the Judson Press editors, and simply could not do my work at Evergreen on an ongoing day-to-day basis. We are truly partners in ministry; I'm grateful for her support every day.

There have been a lot of people who have supported Evergreen over and above. My debt of gratitude for these people and their generosity is beyond mere words. The first of these I must mention is Louise Roberts, the widow of the first Executive Minister of American Baptist Churches of the Northwest. As Evergreen came into being, Louise was dying, but she remembered us in her will. Her gift of almost $35,000 sustained us in our early years, and in fact those dollars are still helping to sustain us! Others gave while they were with us, and it means so much to our ongoing ministry: Al and Harriet Harrington, Richard Ice, Betty Bates, Larry and Fran Nelson, Mabel Brockhoff, and Sylvia Luckie Benefiel. And there are others who continue to support us: Roy Johnson, Jack and Max Sondericker, Carol Tamparo, Marian Voge, Keith and

Bonnie Harding, Willie and Faye Stewart, Doug and Micky Holmes, and Ellis and Karen Keck.

Two others must be mentioned, neither directly a part of Evergreen. Both were nursery school playmates of Yosh Nakagawa. Their friendship was renewed as adults. Herb Tsuchiya, a member of Chinese Baptist Church of Seattle, has supported us monetarily and with his presence often. Akio Yanagihara was a United Methodist who was a staunch supporter of the work of Yosh, particularly through his photography. You would never believe him to be a photographer to look at him, but our early years were chronicled by his wonderful work. We shall always be grateful for his talent. He proudly wore his ABCUSA lapel pin!

Also to be mentioned are my parents, William "Bill" and Sara "Sally" Patton, who have always had my back and supported my ministries in one way or another. With my dad's passing, their monetary support is gone, and even though she has dementia, I know that my mom keeps me in her prayers.

I'm grateful for early readers of this book, primarily Charlie Scalise, Terry Sue Fischer, and Jeff Woods. Others have also helped, early on they gave invaluable feedback and encouragement. I'm grateful for American Baptist Home Mission Societies for their backing through Judson Press. Rebecca Irwin-Diehl was willing to give me a listen and to give this book a platform. Thank you so much!

Introduction

One challenge facing the Christian church today is how to be inclusive—inclusive racially and culturally, inclusive theologically and politically, inclusive socioeconomically, and in any variety of other areas. This challenge is present for the local congregation, as well as denominations and the structures that exist between the local church and the national bodies. While the American Baptist Churches USA (ABCUSA) is theologically and ethnically diverse (with no one ethnic majority), we struggle with how to "do church" in an inclusive manner within our local churches as well as our regional and our national bodies.

The story of the Evergreen Association of American Baptist Churches represents an earnest effort to be faithful to the call for an inclusive body of Christ. The Evergreen Association is a regional body of American Baptist Churches USA. Formally welcomed into the ABCUSA body in 2003, Evergreen is unique in our denominational life for at least two reasons. First, Evergreen is organized by ethnic caucuses (as opposed to geographic) and does its work by consensus (as opposed to the traditional Robert's Rules of Order where majority rules). This atypical organizational structure has facilitated our experiment to do ministry in a manner that respects and includes various ethnic groups, especially those that have been traditionally marginalized.

In large part, this book is about the priceless lessons learned about what many would call "multicultural ministry." Multicultural ministry happens organically, by the mere fact that there are people of different cultures "in the room." On the other hand, "inclusive ministry" requires an intentional effort to ensure that the different cultures are fully present in the room and participate at all levels of decision-making.

This book is a call to all people, especially those in multicultural church organizations, to inclusive ministry using the story of Evergreen Association of American Baptist Churches. There are few stories about other religious bodies and organizations that have navigated well the process of becoming or being inclusive. We have managed to create a regional body of churches that appreciates, advocates, and expects diversity in all we do. This is why Evergreen is a story worth telling.

To tell this story, we will use the metaphor of the feast or the table. Though not a perfect metaphor, I hope it will help keep us all at the table (pun intended) through the wonderfully messy conversation of inclusive ministry.

An Evergreen Story: A Banquet Meal

One of the decisions necessary to make when creating an inclusive table is what food will be served. This seemingly basic decision about the menu can become more complex in a multicultural setting, since food represents a deeply cultural expression. The following story represents how even at the most basic levels, Evergreen has sought to be faithful to the call to be inclusive.

While planning Evergreen's tenth anniversary celebration in 2013, the diverse planning committee decided to have a banquet rather than the simple common meal of previous years. Plans were made to honor the people involved in developing Evergreen: the Task Force, the Vision Committee, and the Transitional Executive Committee. We wanted the event to have flair and a feel that was different from our usual casual dinners at annual meetings.

Japanese Baptist Church was hosting our annual meeting that year. During one meeting of the planning committee, the Japanese Baptist Church representative reported that the group planning the Friday evening meal had decided to have a buffet. The committee expressed concern that a buffet would not be well received since a banquet meal had been advertised.

In a follow-up conversation with the woman responsible for planning the Friday evening meal, I shared the planning committee's concern. She in turn shared her concern that on previous occasions when a traditional Japanese meal was served to a group that included Euro Americans and African Americans, an excessive amount of food was left over. She had concluded that other ethnicities didn't like the meal. I assured her that at banquet meals where food was plated, leftovers were inevitable because people had so little choice about what was put on their plates. After some discussion, we agreed to serve Japanese bento boxes, which included a variety of entrees and sides.

At the event, the pastor, Rev. Jennifer Ikoma-Motzko, introduced the meal in this manner: "Tonight's banquet meal is served as a bento box—a gift of our Japanese American culture and a contribution to our diverse Evergreen family. To celebrate this auspicious occasion, on top of your box is an origami crane. And as an act of inclusiveness, you'll notice we included not just chopsticks but also forks! Inside your box each item of your meal is presented in its own compartment. Every box but the vegan boxes has three entrees—Kobi beef, teriyaki chicken, and shrimp tempura—plus a salad, green beans, California sushi, and, in its own compartment, ginger. Being not just Baptist but also Asian American, one of our love languages in this congregation is food. So we hope you enjoy our culinary gift box, which also happens to make an excellent take-home container for any leftovers you may have!" The bento meal was served, and the banquet was a success.

Why Am I the Author of This Book?

I have been an American Baptist since I was baptized as a child at the First Baptist Church of Temperance, Michigan, a congregation that was then ABCUSA affiliated. During my childhood, the town of Temperance was a WASP (white, Anglo-Saxon, Protestant) community that didn't even have a Catholic church until I was in high school. When I went to Michigan State University, I discovered that there was an entity called American Baptist Churches USA. I was introduced to the denomination through an American Baptist Student Ministry and its full-time campus chaplain.

With the chaplain's encouragement, I attended an American Baptist–related seminary, then Eastern Baptist Theological Seminary (now Palmer Theological Seminary). Upon graduation in 1973 with a Masters of Arts in Religion, I began serving American Baptist congregations. After ten years, I returned to Eastern to earn a Master of Divinity. From there, I felt a call to pursue doctoral studies at Temple University (which has American Baptist roots). Upon earning my doctorate in group dynamics, I was called to be Associate Executive Minister of American Baptist Churches of the Northwest. In this role, I began my work with what was to become Evergreen Association.

When I began, I didn't have any background or formal training in inclusive ministry. I had much to learn. But perhaps it was my greenness that allowed me to help chart a new course for the churches I served. We learned some important principles and lessons in the process, which we hope will be inspirational to others.

Setting the Stage for Telling the Story

For those who are not affiliated with the ABCUSA, it may be helpful to understand our makeup in order to appreciate the ways in which Evergreen represents a departure from the denomination's traditional structure. Today's American Baptist Churches USA is one of the most diverse Protestant denominations in the United States, at least on paper. Paradoxically, it is known in some Christian circles as "mainline" and in other Christian circles as "evangelical." Like all congregations in the Baptist tradition, governance rests with the local church rather than with an elected or appointed leader. We have no common creed but rather state that the Bible is our sole authority.

Although ABCUSA's formal organization is relatively new, its first churches, original regional associations, and mission agencies stem from the oldest Baptist organizations in the United States. One of the first schisms in Baptist life happened over a disagreement about whether or not slave holders would be sent as missionaries. This disagreement led to the organization of the Southern Baptist Convention in the 1840s. In 1907, the American Baptist Mission Societies (Foreign, Home, Education, and Publication) came together to form what is today the American Baptist Churches USA. Though we have gone through several organizational shifts in our hundred-plus year history, we have always retained the identities of the original mission societies and determined how to have a united vision and mission.

One major shift in our structure occurred in the 1970s: the creation of regional organizations that sent representatives to a common national board. Some groups simply changed their names from state or city conventions to regional associations. Others combined entities to form larger regions from some smaller conventions. One of the more radical changes happened in the Northwest where the Washington Baptist Convention, Idaho Baptist Convention, Montana Baptist Convention, and Utah Baptist Association came together to form the American Baptist Churches of the Northwest.

None of the above-named conventions that made up the American Baptist Churches of the Northwest disappeared because they all owned camp properties or leases. But the conventions gave all program and service responsibility to the region of American Baptist Churches of the Northwest (ABC-NW). In addition to the conventions, an organization made up of the American Baptist congregations in the greater Seattle area known as Seattle Baptist Union became a grant-giving organization for the churches and entities in and around a specific geographic area of Seattle.

To help set the context of this work, it is also helpful to know a little bit about how American Baptist Churches work in general. The free-church tradition means that the local church has autonomy in its work, ministry, and mission. There is no confession or creed, no book of order or book of discipline, no other humanly drafted document that every church must follow. Congregations that choose to associate with American Baptist Churches USA do so through regional bodies. Local churches covenant to support their regional association as well as the national organizations, including American Baptist Home Mission Societies, American Baptist International Ministries, and the traditionally designated Office of the General Secretary, which oversees American Baptist Churches USA.

Another organization that played a part in the formation of the Evergreen Association is the Association of Welcoming and Affirming Baptists (AWAB). AWAB was founded as a group of American Baptist congregations that declare that they are fully supportive of LGBTQ (lesbian, gay, bisexual, transgendered, and queer) people's inclusion as full members of the church, as well as committing to being actively involved with the larger LGBTQ community in the city or town they serve.

The Table Metaphor

When I served the American Baptist Churches of the Northwest, one quarter of the approximately two hundred churches was majority non-white in their primary makeup (African American,

Asian American, Native American, or Hispanic American). But when entities of ABC-NW met, it usually looked like all our churches were primarily Euro American in makeup. On many occasions ABC-NW would do a good job of inviting all churches to participate, and some people from non–Euro American churches would come one time, then disappear. At the national American Baptist level, the gatherings too often looked much the same, despite our proclaimed diversity.

I found that, in explaining how American Baptists tend to work out our diversity, it was helpful to use the metaphor of having a feast. In preparing for the feast, the planners invite everyone they know to the meal. They may even intentionally invite a diverse group of people. Everyone who is able comes. After the meal, the guests indicate that they appreciated the invitation and enjoyed the meal. They were good guests; they didn't criticize what was served, how it was served, or anything else about the meal. At the end of the meal, they said thanks and praised the cooks and table preparers. They went home after the meal, just as expected, to return only when another invitation was extended.

ABC-NW and ABCUSA operated similarly. The majority Euro American leaders and congregations decided that an event should happen. They might even invite a "minority" representative or two to join in the planning even though the event had already been scheduled and framed out. If the planning group did it well, invitations were extended to the entire multicultural family. There would be some level of participation from the whole family. After the event, all would return to their home congregations and not connect with one another afterward. The planners may have been praised for a well-prepared, well-served program or event, but ownership of the program or event did not occur, so participation happened only upon invitation to future events.

Evergreen took a different approach in its formation. Everyone was invited to build the table, set the table, decide the menu, and share in the meal. Everyone stayed around for the clean-up and planned for the next meal. Everyone was represented at the vision table; everyone was expected at the Constituting Convention; all were expected to give their voice. As a result, we built ownership into the process.

Many individuals were involved in building Evergreen; one, Yosh Nakagawa, has been invaluable to our work and deserves mentioning from the outset.

Yosh Nakagawa and Evergreen

Evergreen's story is the story of many people, but particularly it is part of the story of Yosh Nakagawa. Evergreen's story is Yosh's story because the birth of Evergreen gave Yosh hope. With that voice, he found the courage to say what was on his heart and mind. You will hear from many voices of Evergreen, but Yosh's voice provides particular meaning and shows most poignantly the impact of our work.

Yosh is a second-generation Japanese American whose parents immigrated to the United States. Yosh does not speak Japanese; his parents did not encourage any of their children to speak the language. His parents ran a small grocery store in the Japanese community of Seattle until they were moved out with their neighbors into an internment camp in 1942. When they were released from the camp, they returned to Seattle where they both found blue-collar jobs, Yosh's mother as a domestic and his father as a gunny sack sorter.

Yosh graduated from Seattle's Garfield High School in 1951 in a widely diverse class that included African Americans, Chinese, Jews, Japanese, Native Americans, and Euro Americans. While visibly diverse, none of his peers learned each other's stories. Yosh, along with a classmate, helped them write their stories during the celebration of the fiftieth anniversary of their graduation.

Yosh attended Linfield College for one year, then continued his undergraduate education for a time at the University of Washington. After graduating, Yosh started out as a custodian with Osborn and Ulland, a sporting goods company in the greater Seattle area. Eventually, the original Norwegian owners bequeathed the company not to their own children but to Yosh, who had become known as the OUKid. He was a gregarious Japanese American (not a trait usually associated with the Japanese), hardworking, and fair-minded. As far as Osborn and Ulland were concerned, he was a Norwegian of Japanese heritage.

During Yosh's work as president of Osborn and Ulland, he was known as someone who encouraged athletes, women as well as men, Asian, Black, Hispanic, and Native as well as Caucasian. He supported the women's athletic program at the University of Washington by being sure that they had equipment and uniforms. He believed that if something was the right thing to do, a way would be found to do it. Yosh was often the vehicle for finding that way. To encourage people to come to Osborn and Ulland, he brought many star athletes to Seattle. If the athletes were African American, he befriended them and connected them to African American churches. He still keeps in touch with the widow of famed African American tennis star Arthur Ashe. Arthur was a friend and mentor to Yosh in part because Yosh was also a tennis player. Though he doesn't ski, Yosh is named on the local skiers' hall of fame because he was a friend to skiers.

Yosh took his conviction that everyone should have a chance into his church as well as into the Japanese American community. He was one of those who determined that it would be a good idea for Japanese Americans who had been interned during World War II to make pilgrimages to the old campsites with their families and friends. He met a good deal of resistance at first, but eventually his people did find it healing to return and to share their history with family and friends.

Yosh became one of the experts who the National Park Service used as they began to open these internment camps around the country. For the first time, the historical sites had experts that were still living—because Yosh insisted that the park service listen to the surviving internees. He refused to work with the parks if they did not comply. That insistence has made those sites far better than they would have been otherwise. For example, one of the things that Yosh remembered about his years at Minidoka Camp near Hunt, Idaho, was playing baseball on one of the camp's several ball fields. One of his dreams was that the Minidoka historical site would have a baseball field. The Park Service said it would take several years to raise the money and put the ball field in, but with Yosh's backing and urging and with the help of many friends, a ball field was dedicated in eighteen months at Minidoka.

For the 2005 Biennial Convention of American Baptist Churches USA, held in Washington DC, Yosh decided to thank American Baptists for their work with the one-hundred-twenty-thousand Japanese Americans during their internment. He worked to put together a large display. He presented pins of the logo of Camp Mindoka to the General Secretary of American Baptist Churches USA, and to the executive directors of the national mission boards, the benefits board, and the American Baptist Historical Society at a special ceremony. Before and after this event he kept asking me, "Do they understand?" I usually replied that they did not understand that the gesture of thanks didn't just come from Baptist Japanese, but all the Japanese, whether they are Buddhist or Catholic or atheist—that they were grateful that people cared. Yosh said, "This thank you came about because of Evergreen!"

Yosh is an active member of Japanese Baptist Church in Seattle. The church had been closed by the US government during World War II and was reopened despite the desire of the white majority that the Japanese should mainstream into US culture after the war. Yosh has served at the church in many capacities. One position he particularly enjoyed was coach of their basketball and volleyball teams. He has served in many volunteer positions: on the board, a term or two as moderator, and unofficially as a spokesperson for his generation in the church. In 1970 Yosh's pastor, Rev. Dr. Paul Nagano, encouraged him to become active in American Baptist Churches USA. The Honorable Charles Z. Smith, a friend and lawyer (who was the first African American layperson to serve as President of American Baptist Churches USA), also encouraged him to become active. After these urgings, Yosh became and remained active for the next forty years. American Baptists loved Yosh's commitment and enthusiasm. He served on three national boards, helped to organize the American Baptist Asian American Caucus, and volunteered in myriad other ways. In 2001, he was elected vice-president of American Baptist Churches USA.

You will see Yosh's name many times in these pages. He's here because he made a difference. However, you won't see his name listed among the officers or committee members with one exception. Yosh would be the first to say that's because he isn't an up-front player; he claims to be the "water boy." But in my experience, Yosh has often acted as coach. When I first began work with Japanese Baptist Church and the other Asian American Baptist Churches in the Seattle area, I asked Yosh to be my teacher. It was one of the best requests I ever made of anyone, and he has not disappointed me.

In 2008, Yosh was told by his doctor to go home and get his affairs in order. He had a diagnosis of cancer. After a regimen of chemo and radiation, he was declared cancer-free and resumed his volunteer work. He figured he had been given a reprieve because he had not yet finished the work he was to do. And he hasn't stopped working. He has labored tirelessly to get the word out about the injustices done to the Japanese during World War II and to encourage all people, especially Host Nations People, to be their best. He often uses sports equipment and his connections to make this happen.

Yosh had another experience with cancer in 2016, and once again he was faced with the possibility that he would not live through the treatment. He went into remission, this time from colon cancer, and is once again building his itinerary of places to go to tell his story and people to see to encourage them on their way. I am always glad to encourage Yosh to do his ministry, to live out his call as best he can with the energy and health God has given him. It is people like Yosh who will make the story of Evergreen live.

True understanding of the Evergreen story requires a look at the perspective of many others. Over the years, people have shared their testimonies about Evergreen in our monthly newsletter. Throughout this volume, you will find sidebars titled "Voices from Evergreen," which feature abridged verses of those testimonies, which I've adapted to give a sense of what a difference the Evergreen experience has made in people's lives. I hope that reading these reflections will give you a better picture of Evergreen.

Of the many folks who had a hand in the birth of Evergreen, no one believes that we did everything perfectly or correctly. I do believe, however, that our attempts to be inclusive were well received for a variety of reasons. Perhaps preeminent among them was that *someone* was making an effort.

Inclusive ministry is messy. That's true whether you're talking about inclusion of diverse cultures and ethnicities, differing theological views, different gender identities and sexual orientations, diverse generations, abilities, or socioeconomic classes. Mess comes with the territory. Although there are a growing number of books about inclusive efforts at ministry, we would still claim that there is no "right" way to go about it. The important thing is to *try.*

Over the years we have been told that our story could be helpful to other Christian organizations and even organizations outside the church. And so here it is, with the prayer that it will indeed be helpful.

The first chapter of the book will consider the meaning of culture and how it impacts the work of the local church and of Evergreen in particular. Chapter 2 dives deeper into culture and examines how our cultural differences sometimes make communications difficult. The third chapter will look at consensus and how it works in Evergreen. Chapter 4 will consider Evergreen's use of caucuses and examine the Developmental Model of Intercultural Sensitivity as we consider the role of caucuses. Chapter 5 will look at the importance of relationships. You will find an excursus at the end which tells the back story of Evergreen. Throughout the book, you will find testimonies from those who have been impacted and have impacted Evergreen. The appendices contain supporting documents such as the Evergreen bylaws.

We hope that in telling Evergreen's story, in sharing what we have come to claim as "the Evergreen Way," others will be inspired to be more inclusive in their ministry or work in their world, so that God's love will be known.

CHAPTER 1

Getting the Table Ready

> If then God gave them the same gift that he gave us when we believed in the Lord Jesus Christ, who was I that I could hinder God? (Acts 11:17)

God's call for the church to be inclusive has its roots in the early church. The above Scripture is the concluding statement the apostle Peter made to the other apostles and Jewish believers in Jerusalem after they heard that Peter had gone to the home of a Gentile God-fearer and eaten with uncircumcised believers.

Jewish custom, based on Mosaic law, said that one was defiled if one ate with an uncircumcised or non-Jewish person. A faithful person absolutely avoided doing so. This ancient law was challenged by the early church. In Acts 10, Peter testified as to why he had done something to break from this custom. He had been praying at a friend's house in Joppa when he had a vision. A large sheet filled with all kinds of animals, including reptiles, beasts of prey, and various birds, came before Peter, and a voice told him to kill and eat. Peter refused because these were not animals that were kosher; they were forbidden as food for God's chosen people according to Deuteronomy and Leviticus. Peter had never eaten these animals before as the dictates of his faith had taught him. In the vision, he was told that what God made clean, he must not call profane. After this happened three times, the sheet disappeared.

At the same time, some men sent by Cornelius (an uncircumcised, faithful Gentile) arrived at the house where Peter was staying. The same Spirit told Peter to go with them. They took Peter and some friends back to Cornelius's home. Cornelius told Peter and his friends that during his prayer time, he had received the command to send for Peter. Then Peter told Cornelius his story, beginning with these words: "I truly understand that God shows no partiality, but in every nation anyone who fears him and does what is right is acceptable to him" (Acts 10:34b-35). He continued to tell the story of Jesus the Christ. Before Peter finished speaking, Cornelius believed, and the Holy Spirit fell upon him and his household.

As Peter concluded his story to those in Jerusalem, he summed up his decision to accept Cornelius and his household as partners with the words, "Who was I that I could hinder God?" (Acts 11:17b). When the believers in Jerusalem heard the whole story from Peter, they were silenced at first, and then they praised God and said, "God has given even to the Gentiles the repentance that leads to life" (Acts 11:18b).

Thus the early church began a cultural shift, from an understanding of a God just for them (the circumcised, monocultural Jewish believer in Jesus) to a God for all (circumcised and uncircumcised, Jew and non-Jew, multicultural). It was a major shift in understanding. It was a change in the culture of the early church. The first Christians had believed their gospel ministry was exclusive to the Jews until God told Peter that Christ's church was inclusive of everyone. And when the Spirit put a person (Cornelius) in Peter's path, Peter discovered that when the community of faith opened itself to the possibility, there was someone right in their midst to expand the church's understanding of the gospel, and especially that God intended it for all.

Acts 11 describes the initial concerns of the council in Jerusalem regarding this change of understanding, and the council's eventual affirmation of Peter's testimony. However, the balance of Acts and the New Testament letters describe ongoing tensions in the early church in dealing with this cultural shift. God's people had to be reminded repeatedly in the early days that Jesus came for everyone, not just for the Jews. For the earliest Christians, understanding this change was not an easy undertaking, even though they evidentially accepted it as part of God's plan. God was clear: the church needed to be inclusive.

More than two thousand years later, we still struggle with what it means to be inclusive in our congregations and ministries. To be clear, no matter what we believe or what we do, God is inclusive. God's love is for everyone. "For God so loved the whole world" and everyone in that world. Too often we have intentionally and unintentionally been exclusive in our worship and our work. Today, many organizations and congregations want to be more inclusive but don't know what steps they need to take to become so. Our hope is that these pages offer some help toward that end.

My Acts 11:17 Moment

After the meeting of the Evergreen Baptist Association on February 22, 2003, when the bylaws were adopted by those present by consensus, Yosh Nakagawa, then vice-president of American Baptist Churches USA, said to me, "For the first time I feel a part of the portrait of the American Baptist family." Yosh, a layman, had been volunteering in American Baptist work for more than thirty years at that time. He enthusiastically, lovingly, and loyally gave of his time. He took Christian values seriously and used them in his work at Osborn and Ulland. How incredible that after thirty years of volunteering and serving for American Baptist Churches locally, regionally, and nationally, he finally felt like he was truly part of the American Baptist family. What a shame that it had taken so long!

This was my Peter moment, my "how could I hinder God?" moment, when I knew that Evergreen had a God-given purpose for being. Yosh's statement was my mandate to take seriously the call to lead Evergreen in the work of inclusion, being sure that all were truly part of the family we claimed to be. Before that moment, I was sure that starting a new region was simply a convenience for ABC-NW to isolate certain churches from the wider regional fellowship. But with Yosh's statement, I understood that God was using this new organization for a more important purpose: to demonstrate and live out inclusive ministry.

Exploring Culture

In order to get the point of being multicultural, we must first examine the meaning of culture.

I once told a multicultural team that all churches are multicultural if they have men and women in them. In reality, culture actually comprises many different expressions that extend far beyond the common assumptions of race and ethnicity.

For example, the town where I grew up was Euro American in makeup, a bedroom community of Toledo, Ohio. First Baptist Church was just a couple of blocks from my home. All the people who went there were white. As churches go, it was monocultural, but not really. It was made up of both people who had lived there all their lives, and people like my parents and myself and older siblings, who had moved there. There were people who were farmers, people who worked in the nearby city, and people who worked in small businesses around town or in nearby industries like my dad. Most mothers did not work outside the home. Most people drove cars, as there was no public transportation available other than school buses. Most of the children went to the public Bedford Township schools. The diversity wasn't apparent or even particularly significant. Yet it was multicultural, if the people examined their differences carefully.

Most marriages in America today are a blending of two cultures. Just ask a couple who share their first Thanksgiving. Should the turkey be roasted, deep-fried, or smoked? If roasted, with what do you stuff the bird (if you do), and what do you call it, "dressing" or "stuffing"? Do you use white bread, wheat bread, cornbread, or rice? Celery or sage? Sausage or oyster or clam? And what are your "must-have" sides—green bean casserole, sweet potato casserole, cranberry salad or cranberry sauce, mashed potatoes, corn casserole, macaroni and cheese, or candied yams? What bread accompanies your Thanksgiving feast—Pillsbury crescent rolls, Parker house rolls, cornbread, or none? And then there is dessert! What is the must-have for your family: pumpkin pie, apple pie, pecan pie, or no pie at all but a particular kind of cake?

Given the sights, sounds, tastes, and smells of Thanksgiving, how do any of us dare proclaim we are a monocultural people? We are all different, and the differences are real, even when preparing a Thanksgiving feast. These kinds of differences are cultural, not just personal preference.

At an Evergreen gathering, it is immediately apparent that you are in a multicultural environment by anyone's definition. A gathering of Evergreen churches looks diverse at a glance; there are Hispanic, black, white, and Asian at most events. Not only are there men and women, but also straight and gay, urban and rural. There are those who were born in many parts of the United States and in different parts of the world. There are clergy and laity who have a variety of occupations, from farmer to computer programmer to stay-at-home parent.

The cultural part of multicultural ministry encompasses many ideas. It consists of what one can see, taste, feel, hear, and smell, the way we dress, the foods we eat, the music we play, and the sports we enjoy. Additionally, culture consists of shared values, the patterns of living, the myths we live out, and our shared beliefs. Together these make up one's culture.

The Iceberg Analogy of Culture

One way to begin to understand culture is to think of an iceberg. An iceberg is a phenomenon of glaciers, rivers, or lakes of ice that slowly flow toward the sea. As the glacier reaches the ocean or sea, chunks break off and become icebergs—huge pieces of what was once a glacier, ice floating on the water. What you see of the iceberg, the part above water, is only about 10 percent of the iceberg. The remaining 90 percent is hidden from sight below the water. The portion below the water extends far beyond and far below what can be seen on top.

Although culture is much more fluid and dynamic than an iceberg, the analogy allows us to understand that a culture isn't just what we can experience with our senses. The majority of culture—patterns, beliefs, values, and myths—are below the water line of the iceberg, the things that cannot be seen or directly sensed (and that we often do not see or easily name in ourselves).

The top of the iceberg—the cultural realties that one can see, touch, smell, hear, and taste—are for the most part objective rather than subjective. These aspects can be more easily taught and changed. One can see generational cultural differences in dress, from something a young person might wear to something a person in his or her eighties might wear, or what a native Hawaiian might wear versus what a native Alaskan might wear. One can also touch differences in cloth, cotton versus silk or deerskin (of the Plains Native American tribes) versus cloth made from cedar bark (of the Northwest tribes). One can hear the differences in culture in the music, generationally or nationally. One can smell and taste the differences in the food offered by different cultures. One can get a flavor of another culture by seeing its customs, trying on the clothes, or eating the food, but a person's own culture will not change when experiencing someone else's. All who eat spaghetti are not Italian, but the food comes from Italy (or long before that, from China). One can eat spaghetti and enjoy it, but doing so doesn't make one Italian. Being Italian has far more to do with the below-the-iceberg stuff of values, beliefs, myths, and patterns—just as being any nationality involves much more than a menu.

Consider as an example the story of the woman who, when preparing a ham, always cut a bit off both ends before she baked it. A friend asked her why she did this. The woman said she did not know, except her mother always did. The woman asked her mother and got the same reply; she did it because her mother always had. The good news was the grandmother was still alive. So daughter and granddaughter went to her and asked, "Why do we always cut both ends off a ham before putting it in the oven?" "Well," the grandmother said, "I don't anymore because I got a bigger oven and a bigger pan. When I was cooking as a young mother, we only had a small oven and a small pan, so in order for the ham to fit, I had to cut a little off. I always figured it was better to cut a little off both ends than to cut a huge piece off one end." The grandmother had no idea she had passed along this cooking quirk, and her daughter and granddaughter had no idea why they cooked a ham this way. Maybe there isn't always a good reason to do something in a particular way—except that we've *been* doing it that way.

We have specific cultures in our congregations, too. Some are things easily experienced because they are "above the surface." The songs we sing, the clothes most of the attendees wear, the time services are held—all can be hints as to the culture of a congregation.

If I am meeting with American Baptists who have been in the church for many years, and I suggest singing the Doxology, most will join me with the traditional words and tune. Nonbelievers would have no idea what *doxology* means, let alone know a tune and words that go with it. Increasingly these days, even the traditional Doxology is not universally known by believers, as more and more churches have changed words and/or tune from what was once more universal among many of us.

Churches have their own ways of doing things. Some cultural traditions take shape within certain ethnic contexts. For example, one of the traditions in the African American church after the sermon is a call to have those who have made a decision for Christ or who want to join the church to come forward. The phrase used to indicate the timing for this practice is "the doors of the church are now open." Those familiar with the culture of the African American church understand that this is the time for making your intentions known by coming up to the front of the church, where deacons or other church leaders are usually waiting to greet you.

In one predominantly African American church seeking to become multicultural, the tradition of "opening the doors of the church" did not have a shared meaning among those unfamiliar with the tradition. Therefore, a pastor was surprised that when he "opened the doors of the church" many people would get up and leave the sanctuary as if the service was over. After talking with some folks, he realized the phrase was misunderstood to mean that the service had concluded, the time had come to go home, the doors of the church were open so people could leave! A common expression used and understood in the African American church community had a different meaning outside the community.

Our "below the water line of the iceberg" cultural values, beliefs, patterns, and myths are often difficult to discover and change. Because we are often unaware of our below-the-surface cultural realities, we may end up in cultural clashes with others.

Culture Clash

When any two people meet, it's possible that their patterns of life will clash. Culture clashes can happen over things big or small. And what might be big to one might seem small to the other and vice versa. The more they share the same beliefs, myths, patterns, and values, the less likely a culture clash.

It is often these below-the-surface, unexamined, unknown cultural realties that cause clashes between individuals, between different cultural groups, and even within groups. Neither groups nor individuals spend much time examining their values, beliefs, patterns, and myths. Clashes occur because we often universalize our way of doing things as *the* way of doing things.

My work with congregations in transition provides an example. One of my jobs is to help churches when a pastor leaves. When working with pastoral search committees, I encourage them to spend a good deal of time getting to know their church's culture on a much deeper level than they ever have before. I tell them that a pastoral search is prime time to "mine the iceberg." The better the search committee knows the church, the better it can be at finding a pastor who is a good fit. The failure to learn a congregation's culture while seeking new leadership can prove disastrous. One church in a Navy town in Washington state called a pastor who had never been in the military or even been out of West Virginia. It was a pastoral relationship that did not survive. After just a few months, the pastor and his family gladly went back to West Virginia. If the church had done a better job of knowing themselves, the mismatch might not have happened, and the resulting pain may have been avoided.

A church's failure to pay attention to its own culture, or one that views its culture one way while others view it differently, can be problematic. The church that determines, for example, to have an English as a Second Language program, but there are no non-English speaking people in the church or its neighborhood, has not examined its culture. The church that is better at claiming and sharing its unique culture tends to be better at attracting people. The church that thinks it can be open to everyone oftentimes discovers that it is a comfortable fit only for those who have been a part of the congregation for a long time already. It is one thing to desire to shift one's culture to attract youth or diverse groups, for example, but before this can happen, a church must be acutely aware of its congregation's current culture.

An Evergreen Story

A Change in Structure

From the beginning, Evergreen sought to do business differently. While we did not set out to do so, our work represented a cultural shift in the ABCUSA, beginning with the way we organized. This included the way in which we chose our name. Normally, American Baptist churches are organized by regions, which generally have distinct geographical boundaries. In May 2002, Evergreen was deliberate in choosing the name of the organization to contain the name *association*. We believed that choosing the word *association* reflected our desire for relationships to be a core value in our work.

Another preliminary decision occurred in February 2003 when we adopted bylaws that organized us by ethnic caucuses that made decisions by consensus. No one was accustomed to working in this manner. Truth be told, the few of us who thought we knew what work by caucus and consensus meant still had no idea how to implement such a process. We hadn't a

Establishing Relationships

Building a relationship with "the other" is the first step toward inclusion. We can't just say, "*You* are welcome to *our* table." That is hospitality but not full inclusion because the table is very much "ours," which means we chose the seating arrangements, the menu, the table settings, and the etiquette for our table. In contrast, the work of intentional inclusion must be demonstrated from the beginning of the relationship by including as many as possible in the decision-making process. Building relationships is important for relationships' sake, without setting an agenda, without seeking a particular outcome.

clue how this way of doing business would look in terms of the day-to-day operations of Evergreen. But our shared faith in God gave us the courage to go down paths and make decisions that, though outside our comfort zone and expertise, we believed would best help us to reach our desired outcome—a truly inclusive ministry.

In June 2003 the Evergreen Association was welcomed as a region in the American Baptist Churches USA. And to our surprise, some churches located outside our region wanted to join us. While we were gratified that others saw our new way as viable, we felt too unsure of ourselves to invite others who had not been part of our history to join us. It was important for us to figure out who we were and how we were going to operate before having other people or congregations join us. So paradoxically, this new, radical organization that sought to be inclusive did not immediately welcome churches outside ABC Northwest to its fold, but rather took time to establish and understand the new culture being created.

To advance the notion of building relationships, it is important to show genuine interest in others and to become as comfortable as possible with them. Once a genuine relationship is established, an overture might be made to become part of building a new community together, and a greater willingness to be involved may result.

When I first came to the Northwest, I served as area minister. Of the forty or so churches for which I was responsible, ten were primarily African American. I started visiting the churches on Sunday mornings. In some of the African American churches, I was invited to sit in the pulpit, a gesture of honor toward a visiting clergyperson. Others did not invite me because they had a practice of not allowing women in the pulpit. I continued the practice of periodically visiting all of the congregations.

One cultural clash occurred when one church (which did not have women in the pulpit) invited me and another church (which *did* allow women in their pulpit) to a special service, hosted by both congregations. People from the latter church were disturbed that I had not been invited to the pulpit during the service. Although I was not offended, understanding it to be a cultural issue, it *was* a problem for people in the guest congregation—a culture clash between two similar but not identical cultures.

Over time my presence was not only noted but counted on by the African American churches. I knew my visitation had done some good when I started getting invitations to attend special services and community events. I knew I was beginning to be accepted by the community when I was invited to speak at the homegoing service for one long-time pastor. Building relationships does make a difference.

One of our continuing mantras (beliefs) from the early days of

Voices of Evergreen

Rev. James Winbush was chair of the ABC-NW New Region Task Force, and is currently an associate pastor at New Beginnings Christian Fellowship. He gave this testimony in July 2013.

The Evergreen Association is the youngest region of the American Baptist Churches USA. Who would have known that Evergreen would have such an impact on the local, regional, and national scene? We were born out of the core elements of fear, self-righteousness, and the assumption of privilege. We moved forward from those experiences. We were unsure of what we would become, but we were sure

Evergreen is "it is all about relationships." And that conviction holds true today. When we spend time with one another, when we do our relationship-building work, Evergreen is stronger. We have a lot of friends beyond the "boundaries" of Evergreen. People who are not members of any of the churches of the Association call us friends. Some of these friends are people of American Baptist caucuses who understand that our work gives them more visibility in the ABCUSA. Some of them are members of minority groups outside the American Baptist circle who understand that what we are doing may bring hope to what they are doing in their faith group. These friendships didn't happen overnight but after we intentionally cultivated relationship with them.

Questions for Reflection

God calls us to build tables of inclusion. Culture permeates everything in our personal lives and in our collective lives. The first step

of what we did not want to become. Out of this was birthed a model that is inclusive, a model that allows all to be involved.

The caucus model and our willingness to do business by consensus is at the center of the Evergreen experience. This allows a continual sense of fellowship and peace, which leads to collaborative and effective ministry programs. Evergreen is unique because our ministerial events and programs are made up of those who look like the community, not just in leadership but also as workers. In this, Evergreen can continue to be a blessing, both in its model and in the way it conducts business—a blessing by being inclusive. So we strive to continue to be faithful, and we are thankful.

is to know our own culture. Some of the questions we need to answer to explore our own culture include the following:

1. How would we describe the culture of our congregation?
2. What are our values?
3. Do we really value inclusion?
4. If so, how do our programming and use of other resources reflect inclusion?
5. How does our inclusion of children during our worship reflect how we value them (or not) as members of our congregation and faith community?

Voices of Evergreen

Chrystal Cooper, a member of First Baptist Church of Mountlake Terrace, Washington, was selected by the Euro-American-majority churches of Seattle Baptist Union to be on the Vision Committee. Chrystal's reflection was first shared in November 2013.

Twelve years ago I was invited to join a team to help create what would become the Evergreen Association. After much prayer, I said yes, not knowing how long it would take, what I would learn, and how far out of my comfort zone it might take me. At our first meeting, for the first time ever, I was with people from ethnic and cultural backgrounds different from mine. Although I felt overwhelmed and didn't know what to expect, I knew that we all shared our faith in Christ and the comfort that God would lead us through this journey.

As we began our work, we intentionally got to know one another and discover ways in which we were alike, instead of

6. What beliefs do we have that might create barriers to our becoming an inclusive ministry?

7. What are our beliefs? Not just the obvious one of being followers of Jesus the Christ, but our beliefs about church policy, structure, women in ministry, youth leadership, and so on? Which of our beliefs might create barriers to inclusion?

8. If we are ready to be inclusive, who is currently being excluded? Are we willing to first build relationships with the excluded? Do we understand the culture of the excluded groups? What would have to shift about our culture for us to appeal to excluded groups? In what ways can we begin to embrace the culture of

just seeing the obvious differences. I felt a sense of wonder, excitement, and a bit of fear of the unknown. As we talked about the decisions facing us (name, mission statement, constitution, etc.), I learned so much about viewing issues from different perspectives and through the eyes of others. We agreed that everyone should have equal voice, regardless of church or caucus size. We didn't want to be bound by geography. Our mission had to include the local church, the association, and the world. Our name, Evergreen (because Washington state is nicknamed the Evergreen state), represents long life, change, vitality, and strong roots. Though some of our discussions were lengthy and emotional, we all felt our final decisions were right. Each step fit together so well.

I am so grateful to have been part of shaping Evergreen. I have grown, and my comfort zone has increased. I made new friends and have been proud to see Evergreen grow. We will always be a work in progress as we travel this journey with God and one another.

those different from ourselves (trying the food, learning the language, etc.)?

Voices of Evergreen

Marjorie Burns is a member of Grace Baptist Church, San Jose, California, and a Euro American Association member who served on the executive committee. Below is her testimony, given in July 2008.

In October 2003 my husband, Lloyd, and I visited the Evergreen Association at its inaugural annual meeting. We had been asked by our pastor to attend the meeting to get our impressions of the group and if it felt right for our California-based church. How refreshing it was to be part of a group that encouraged people to participate and speak their minds! Even though we were visitors there to observe, we were included in the conversations.

We saw firsthand how organizing around caucuses gave each group a voice. Decision-making by consensus gave each individual in the caucus a chance to be heard and to be comfortable with the final decision. This was all very new to us, and it felt good! Evergreen folks confessed that it was all new to them as well. They knew why we were there, and they were transparent in explaining that, because this was their first annual meeting, they were not yet ready to accept new churches. That was alright with us. We were willing to wait. It gave a chance for others from Grace Baptist to form their own opinions.

We were delighted when, two years later in 2005, we were accepted and welcomed into the fellowship of the Evergreen Association of American Baptist Churches.

CHAPTER 2

Culture and Communications at the Table

> Now you are the body of Christ and individually members of it. (1 Corinthians 12:27)

In this chapter we will consider the reality of working with differences in the church. We will take a brief look at how respecting differences can allow good to happen. We will consider the work of Geert Hofstede in working with others, looking specifically at the scales of Individualism and Conflict Avoidance. As in the last chapter, we will draw examples from Evergreen and the journey we have taken in multicultural ministry.

> Indeed, the body does not consist of one member, but of many. If the foot would say, "Because I am not a hand, I do not belong to the body," that would not make it any less a part of the body. And if the ear would say, "Because I am not an eye, I do not belong to the body," that would not make it any less a part of the body. If the whole body were an eye, where would the hearing be? If the whole body were hearing, where would the sense of smell be? But as it is, God arranged the members in the body, each one of them, as he chose. If all were a single member, where would the body be? As it is, there are many members, yet

> one body. The eye cannot say to the hand, "I have no need of you," nor again the head to the feet, "I have no need of you." On the contrary, the members of the body that seem to be weaker are indispensable, and those members of the body that we think less honorable we clothe with greater honor, and our less respectable members are treated with greater respect; whereas our more respectable members do not need this. But God has so arranged the body, giving the greater honor to the inferior member, that there may be no dissension within the body, but the members may have the same care for one another. If one member suffers, all suffer together with it; if one member is honored, all rejoice together with it. —1 Corinthians 12:14-26

As we work in the local church to be unified as described in 1 Corinthians 12, recognizing the gifts each of us brings to building God's church can be a struggle. As the writer of 1 Corinthians so clearly indicates, we need one another in all of our unique individuality, but too often we look for sameness. We try to put aside or dismiss our differences. We exert every effort to make others in our image, often assuming that others think as we do. This is not unusual. Groups usually struggle before they are able to work together and work well. The length of time it takes for groups to function effectively differs from group to group. It is not automatic, no matter what the group.

Best-selling author M. Scott Peck, in his book *The Different Drum,* describes characteristics of well-functioning groups. One of the characteristics he names is a "spirit."[1] Peck describes the "spirit" as peace and love that is not created solely by the group itself. I have, as Peck, experienced that spirit as the Holy Spirit, the work of God among a group, leading us to work together well. This includes listening well and accepting the gifts of all in the group. The Spirit of God is at work in the church when it does work well.

Certainly, in the church we need to be open to the work of the Spirit, and part of that openness is to figure out how to recognize the giftedness in one another and put that giftedness to work, not just for the church's benefit but for the well-being of the world.

Our best work as a church is done when we can come together, with the help of the Holy Spirit, and appreciate the other. When we are building a table of fellowship and discipleship in the church, it is important to keep in mind that we don't all think alike (even if we agree theologically), speak alike (even if we agree sociologically), or act alike (even if we agree what might need to be done). Having acceptance and appreciation for how others might think, speak, and act is very important to being able to do inclusive work well. One doesn't have to act, think, or speak the way of the other, but one must have respect for, if not understanding of, the different ways of acting, thinking, and speaking to move the work forward.

We do not need to delay the work by insisting on total understanding of another's way of thinking. Although this is a noble hope, I contend that we can start with respecting one another without necessarily understanding fully the position of the other. With this mutual respect, we can begin to move forward.

A Word about Generalizations

Before proceeding, I need to say a word about generalizations. In discussions about people and cultures, I will make many general statements about a church, a group of churches, an ethnic culture, or perhaps a generation. These statements are not meant to imply that every individual in the group expresses himself or herself in the way I describe, but that the group exhibits a pattern. If I take a general statement and apply that attribute (whether positive or negative) to every (or nearly every) person in a group, it becomes a stereotype. Although I will make many generalizations in these pages, I have no intention of implying that the statements apply to everyone in a group, nor do I intend to imply that an attribute which I assign to a group should be used to denigrate, limit, or negate a group or a person.

It is impossible to discuss culture without making some generalizations, but it is unfair to assume that any generalization is true of all people. For example, I'm a baby boomer because I was born between the years 1946 and 1964. Many books have been written about the baby-boomer generation. While I do have some of the traits of a baby-boomer, I do *not* have many others. When I make generalizations, it is to help us look at how we might better understand another group or even another person, but we should not be surprised when a group or a person exhibits behavior outside what might be considered their generational, sexual, or cultural norm.

An Evergreen Story

In the first years of Evergreen, I spent a lot of time explaining what we were doing to be intentionally inclusive. We had two people from each ethnic caucus on the executive committee, deliberately rotating the role of chairperson from caucus to caucus, and we defined a quorum as having at least one person from every caucus in the room. In response people of color would say to me, "Wow! You are serious about having everyone at the table!" They understood these commitments as providing opportunities for them as ethnic minorities to make a difference in decision-making, rather than being mere "tokens" at the table.

In the very early days of Evergreen, the McKee Consultation was meeting in Seattle. The McKee Consultation is a gathering of African American national and regional leaders in American Baptist Churches.[2] Yosh Nakagawa heard that this group was to meet in Seattle, and as a leader of the Asian Caucus, he invited them to a meal at his favorite Japanese restaurant. This had never happened to the McKee Consultation; no other group had hosted them at a meal before. They had a great time! A few years later, when the Asian Caucus had their first convocation in Tukwila, Washington, a suburb of Seattle, the Evergreen Black Caucus decided to provide a barbeque lunch for them—freshly grilled ribs and chicken, with all the fixings. The Asian Caucus was amazed at the hospitality. At this their first such event, the Asian Caucus had no expectations, so being treated to a meal by the Evergreen Black Caucus was a surprise. The meal offered by each host was a bit out of the other's comfort zone, not part of their cultural norm, but the hospitality extended was extraordinary.

A number of years after that, another wonderful moment took place during a meeting of the Sacred Action on Racism Team, a group put together after the Black Caucus had passed a resolution calling for "sacred action against racism." I gave staff support in the early days of the team, which consisted of a white retired male pastor, an Asian male layperson (our friend Yosh), and an African American deacon. We invited the Rev. Dr. Leslie Braxton (an African American male pastor) to join us for the meeting because we thought we wanted to write a publication on the subject, and we believed he could help us. At one point, Yosh, wanting to make it clear that racism was not just a black and white issue, talked about his incarceration as a youth. He also talked about how his community had a pilgrimage each year from Seattle to the Minidoka site in Idaho. Everyone on the team expressed a desire to go on one of these annual pilgrimages. In Yosh's words, "Even if they never come, just the fact that they said they did want to come was beautiful."

Many years later, because of different circumstances but in response to an invitation, Yosh went to Atlanta, Georgia, to the Ebenezer Baptist Church (old and new), and to the Martin Luther King Jr. sites nearby. He was escorted on this trip by a close friend of the King family, Rev. Dr. Albert Brinson, an American Baptist. Yosh was thrilled to see so much there that spoke of equality for all, including Asians, and to see quotes from Japanese Americans.

This happened in part because Dr. Brinson had come to Seattle and had gone to Bainbridge Island, where there is a touching memorial commemorating the day when the Japanese people were forced off the Island and put behind barbed wire for the duration of World War II. Dr. Brinson understood the connection. He had long known the breadth of the inclusive message of his mentor and friend, Rev. Dr. Martin Luther King Jr.

These are amazing stories because the African American and Asian American cultures are not necessarily alike; in fact, generally they are quite different. Have you ever been to a barbeque where chopsticks were offered? Neither have I! But the appreciation of the Asian Caucus for the barbeque offered by the Black Caucus of Evergreen was overwhelming, and no one asked for chopsticks. On the other hand, while the McKee Consultation members did their best with chopsticks in sharing the meal at the Japanese restaurant, most ended up using forks. They also found Kobe beef delicious, as well as a lot of the other Japanese foods.

Dr. Brinson testified about his experience at the Bainbridge Island Memorial, expressing his appreciation for the friendships he had forged with the Japanese-American people, especially those who had taken him to see the memorial. Yosh couldn't be there that day, but he later received the invitation to go to Atlanta. The connection between Albert Brinson, Yosh, and Japanese Baptist Church is strong because of shared history and understanding. This doesn't mean that Japanese Baptists shout *amen!* during sermons. Nor does it mean Ebenezer Baptist Church in Atlanta serves barbeque with chopsticks. The differences between the African American and Asian American cultures are real and mutually honored. Similarly, there are differences between Euro and Hispanic cultures and among all of the different cultures that make up our society.

We are different people and we have different perspectives and different ideas about the world and about what our communities need. It is a mistake to see everyone as the same and not appreciate the differences we have and the different perspectives we bring to any table where we work. These differences are to be respected, and when we work to bridge differences, we can make real connections with one another. Too often we invite different voices to the table but then fail to listen to the different perspectives there. Too often Euro Americans expect everything to be done "our way," according to our customs and traditions. We generalize our perspective as being the *only* perspective and expect others to endorse us. We are often challenged by how to listen, let alone understand a different way or perspective.

Cultural Differences and Power

Chapter 1 contained a discussion of culture—the culture we can see, taste, smell, touch, and hear, and the below-the-surface culture of patterns, myths, beliefs, and values. We also considered how power differs among cultural groups and reflects these deeply held values, patterns, myths, and beliefs that exist beneath the surface.

Power Distance

Renowned cultural theorist Geert Hofstede, in his seminal work on culture[3] and the workplace, has determined that countries maintain differing values with respect to several dimensions that influence how we approach and engage in work. One such dimension is "power distance." Power distance is defined as the extent to which the less powerful members of institutions and organizations expect and accept that power is distributed unequally.[4] The foundation of this dimension is that all individuals in societies are not equal; power distance expresses the attitude of the culture towards these inequalities among us.

In a highly hierarchical culture, the people at the bottom of the hierarchy expect and accept that they do not hold the power, but that power is held by a ruler and ruling class different from theirs.

In a less hierarchical society, people at the bottom believe that there is a pathway to get power, and that being without power forever is not necessarily a given. This difference in beliefs about power makes a profound difference in how people work with one another and with those whom they perceive as powerful in their system.

We don't often talk about power in the church, let alone power distance. Yet both exist in the church just as in any other institution. In free-church traditions such as American Baptists (essentially a low-power-distant culture), the congregational polity dictates that the local church has the power to determine its own destiny. Consequently, it is assumed that power is distributed equally, or that even the less powerful members of the church can effect real change. However, because we each bring to our work in the church many of the values of our native cultures, the failure to examine how cultural differences impact perceptions of power even among us can lead to conflict.

For example, in many Asian, Hispanic, and African American churches, power is assumed to reside with the pastor without question, and the pastor is assumed to behave in appropriate ways, knowing what the people need and responding to those needs. These assumptions about power can create significant conflict when a congregation seeks to become more multicultural in its membership and leadership. Sometimes when a white pastor is called to an Asian or Hispanic congregation and doesn't understand this dynamic, he or she may be surprised at the power the congregants give the pastor or may be surprised at what the pastor is expected to know about the needs of congregants.

Understanding where power lies and our ability to influence that power can be difficult. In fact, experiences with and perceptions of power can be so deeply hidden that we don't know the difference until we try to influence a leader in the church. Whether we feel we can change the way things are done significantly influences how we operate in the church. If we feel that we can make a difference, we are more likely to speak up and believe that we will be heard. If we feel that we cannot make a difference, that the leaders alone will decide, we are more likely to remain silent in the work of the church.

A Personal Story

This is my honest confession, as a Euro American, working with my dear friend and colleague Yosh Nakagawa. I grew up in a very low-power-distant culture, while Yosh grew up in a more high-power-distant culture. As a result, I must listen differently to Yosh and be aware that he comes from a different culture with a different understanding of hierarchy than I do. Yosh always defers to me because I am the executive minister, even when he is trying to drive home a point about how Asian culture works. For Yosh, driving home a point is achieved in a very indirect manner.

In a high-power-distant culture, the leaders have access to what is occurring throughout their culture. Thus, Yosh assumes I have these connections and resources. He often asks me questions about what "people in the ABC" think about an action he may take or what "people in Evergreen" think about something. He expects, since I am a person with power, I will know the answer to these questions. He is always surprised if I tell him that leaders in the ABC do not particularly care what action he takes. He is surprised because in his mind he is in their "territory." But in our low-power-distant Euro American minds, he is not understood as a threat, especially as a member of the laity. He can go places and have conversations that I cannot necessarily have because of our differences in "perceived power."

Those perceptions are different in the general American culture and his more Asian cultural upbringing. He exercises respect where we don't expect it. He assumes leaders will pay attention to the needs of the laity, even when we don't always (sometimes to our peril).

Individualism and Collectivism

Another scale that Hofstede uses to measures cultural differences is the individualism/collective scale. He explains it as follows:

> The fundamental issue addressed by this dimension is the degree of interdependence a society maintains among its members. It has to do with whether people's self-image is defined in terms of "I" or "We." In Individualist societies people are supposed to look after themselves and their direct family only. In Collectivist societies, people belong to "in groups" that take care of them in exchange for loyalty.[5]

When working with one another, the degree to which a culture maintains interdependence can influence how different cultures communicate ideas. Generally speaking, when a Euro American is thinking about the "common good," he or she still views it from the perspective of an individual: "What's good for one is good for all." On the other hand, the Japanese perceive the "common good" solely as it impacts the entire community; any individual concern is taken out of the equation. The same is true of many other nationalities.

Cultural differences about interdependence have impacted my work in Evergreen. Because of his collective mindset, Yosh asks about the impact of Evergreen on everyone. His questions reflect a concern for the whole. Does the collective body understand what we are doing yet? Do they understand the work of the caucus model? Do they understand how much a difference caucuses make? He thinks collectively about American Baptists or Seattle's Japanese American community or even a sports group. This kind of collective thinking is hard for me to understand. I don't realize how much the collective doesn't see the individual because I see the collective through my individual lens.

Uncertainty Avoidance Index

Also worth our attention here is Hofstede's Uncertainty Avoidance Index (UAI). He defines UAI this way:

> [UAI is] the way that a society deals with the fact that the future can never be known and considers the question of whether we should try to control the future or just let it happen. This ambiguity brings with it anxiety which diverse cultures have learned to deal with in different ways. The extent to which the members of a culture feel threatened by ambiguous or unknown situations and have created beliefs and institutions that try to avoid uncertainty is reflected in the UAI score.[6]

Furthermore, Hofstede states:

> At 92 Japan is one of the most uncertainty avoiding countries on earth. This is often attributed to the fact that Japan is constantly threatened by natural disasters from earthquakes, tsunamis (this is a Japanese word used internationally), typhoons, and volcano eruptions. Under these circumstances, the Japanese learned to prepare themselves for any uncertain situation. This goes not only for the emergency plan and precautions for sudden natural disasters but also for every other aspect of society. You could say that in Japan anything you do is prescribed for maximum predictability. From cradle to grave, life is highly ritualized and you have a lot of ceremonies.[7]

The United States, on the other hand, scores a 46, considerably lower than Japan.[8]

The UAI dimension manifests itself in the way that Yosh and I work. Yosh is going to know what everyone is thinking before a meeting because he has talked to everyone about the agenda ahead of time.

In contrast, I am much more likely to "go with the flow." I do want to know if something major is brewing, but I figure I can deal with general questions and concerns in the moment. Yosh doesn't do "in the moment," certainly not when it comes to decision-making.

Yosh's way can be very helpful when working on consensus-building. He will know if he has consensus before the meeting even happens. It took me a long time to understand this difference between us. We non-anxious avoidance types are less likely to scope out the landscape. Yosh has shown me that scoping out the landscape can be helpful to the process.

Communication Styles

A fourth dimension of difference identified by Hofstede is communication styles. The **direct** communication style is reflected in statements like, "let your *yes* be yes and your *no* be no"[9] or "get to the point." The **indirect** communication style is reflected in the belief that being direct is disrespectful. An indirect communicator would instead tell a story or make assumptions about what has transpired based on what the other person has not said as well as what he or she has said. Euro Americans tend to be direct-communication-style speakers, while many Asian and Native American cultures tend to use indirect communication styles.[10] These differences in communication styles can often result in instances of complete miscommunicating.

Yosh and I often experience this difference in communication styles. More than once, it is only after I reflect on a conversation with Yosh that I think I understand what he has said. I often check with him afterward by asking, "Is this what you meant by that conversation?" Usually, I get a story in reply.

Hofstede's Theory in Action

All of these differences can make for a lively meeting or a frustrating one. Although we were not aware of Hofstede's theories,

Evergreen sought to make a more egalitarian room by giving every church equal voice. We wanted to ensure that the differences in power dynamics did not keep anyone from being heard. We kept this in mind when developing our bylaws.

At the first meeting to read through the proposed bylaws, held at Seattle First Baptist Church (a primarily Euro American church, the largest membership in the Euro Caucus and highest-giving church in the Association), one of the items considered was the number of delegates each church could send to an Association annual meeting. Number of delegates determine number of votes and therefore impact influence and power. Our starting point was bylaws that gave voting rights similar to ABCUSA, which provided for more delegates for churches with more numbers and more delegates to churches with higher mission giving. At our first meeting, this was questioned—and ultimately changed.

The largest primarily African American churches suggested that representation should be the same no matter how many members a church had, and others in attendance agreed. One of the highest-giving primarily Euro American churches suggested that it should not matter how much a church gave; as long as the church gave to American Baptist mission, the number of delegates ought to be the same. Those present agreed to this change. In the end, it was decided that every church in good standing (that gave to American Baptist mission and participated in Evergreen work), no matter their size, could send five delegates to an annual meeting. Adding these criteria to the caucus representative structure was our way of balancing the power, establishing an equality that was new to the churches of Evergreen.

Another provision in Evergreen's bylaws that has helped create a table of equality involves the way we establish quorums. Instead of there being a specific number, quorums are to be established if every seated caucus is represented. In other words, in order to do business on any level, a representative from each caucus must be present. No business decision is valid without everyone being represented.

An Evergreen Story

We stumbled upon our caucus structure and consensus decision-making in part by listening to the differences among us. We do our best work when we look for and embrace our differences. This often sounds uncomfortable to many, but it is the way forward; it is adaptive work rather than technical work. Technical work is taking action that we know how to do, which is usually linear, anticipating that certain actions usually bring certain results. Adaptive work is action that is unknown and untried. The rules for it are not clear, and it often has unintended consequences. It is adaptive because it changes the way things are generally done. While it is difficult to tell others how to go about engaging in adaptive work, finding commonalities is not always best. Rather, in adaptive work we must embrace our differences. We must find the unique way rather than a familiar way. We have often found that this is God's way.

The day came when I knew there was hope for Evergreen and its work. In the first year of Evergreen, we sought to flesh out our mission statement and develop a vision statement. Our mission statement reads: "Being a culturally diverse people who are one in Christ and who value the liberties of our American Baptist heritage, the Evergreen Association of American Baptist Churches will build bridges between communities; provide resources to equip member churches to share Christ and teach God's word; and translate our unity to the world."

We held a day-long meeting as part of this process at the Fremont Baptist Church. The first part of the day, which included Bible study, group-building events, and brainstorming, was done in groups that were intentionally ethnically mixed. At the end of the meeting, we broke into caucuses.

In these early days we really had very little knowledge of how to work across cultures. As caucuses were busy with an assignment that had been given them, the Asian Caucus worked quietly in one corner while both the Euro and Black Caucuses were more vocal in their work. As time went along, one member of the Euro Caucus leaned back and shouted over to the Black Caucus that they were awfully loud. Someone from the Black Caucus immediately responded, "Well, that's how we do our work, so get used to it!" Everyone laughed. That exchange confirmed in me a sense of hope for the work we were trying to do. Rather than backing down to what someone wanted or said from the Euro Caucus, the Black Caucus immediately stated who they were. This had not happened before, but it has happened in many different ways since—a caucus by action, word, or deed saying "we do things this way" without apology being made or expected.

The Body of Christ

First Corinthians 12 describes that, for the church to work well, we need everyone and everyone's diverse gifts. Humans do not easily come to value the gifts of one another, but with practice and determination, listening and work, we can do the work that honors God. The work of the church demands that we value everyone's differences and their gifts. The work of the church demands that we take the time to bring everyone on board, not assuming that everyone thinks or act as I do. It often requires courage; it always involves listening well to others.

The beautiful Corinthian passage quoted at the beginning of this chapter paints a picture of a body and speaks of how the body must depend on all of its different parts. It asks the reader to imagine

Voices of Evergreen

Rev. Walter Heyman is pastor of New Walk Christian Church. He was Evergreen's first General Board Representative. He is now retired from work in Seattle City government. He shared this testimony in 2013.

My journey with the Evergreen Association has been and continues to be a large part of my Christian growth. When Evergreen was conceived ten years ago, I was asked to be its first General Board representative. Like many others, I got caught up in the controversy over what Evergreen represented. I was so focused on theology that I was blinded to its purpose: ministry. I learned that doing ministry is about what's being done for God, not who's doing it. God uses whom God will to build the kingdom.

different parts of the body proclaiming that they didn't need other parts of the body and concludes how ridiculous that would be. In the church, we often forget and sometimes even dismiss parts of our body. The work of inclusive ministry requires us to put aside assumptions about how things are done, especially if things are done a certain way because we've always done it that way!

Questions for Reflection

Some questions to ask of oneself as you prepare to do multicultural work:

1. How am I ready to embrace differences in others?
2. How am I ready to listen?
3. How am I ready to work toward understanding the way of another culture, withholding all judgment to rightness?

I learned to experience ministry through a biblical perspective—and that ministry is about relationships. Through those relationships we can find common ground to serve God together. Biblical ministry destroys the divisions between winners and losers, majorities and minorities, those whose voices are heard and those whose voices are not loud enough to hear. It places all people at the same table, with the same rights and authority. That makes doing ministry a lot more effective and fun.

When asked, "What has Evergreen meant to me?" I would say it has been one of the most important times in my life for change from who I was to who God wants me to be. God always puts us in a place that will set us on the path that God wants us to follows. Evergreen is the place that God used to set my path.

"I thank God for Evergreen—and for what it represents in serving God and building God's kingdom!"

4. How am I ready to embrace the giftedness in others, even if it is a gift that I don't understand?

5. How am I ready to pray for courage?

6. How am I ready to explore and to adapt to another culture's way of doing things?

CHAPTER 3

Consensus

> If then there is any encouragement in Christ, any consolation from love, any sharing in the Spirit, any compassion and sympathy, make my joy complete: be of the same mind, having the same love, being in full accord and of one mind. (Philippians 2:1-2)

Paul writes the Philippians asking them to make his joy complete, being in full accord and one mind. How many pastors would write this? Many, I think! Many a denominational leader desires to write the same to churches. We all desire this unity of mind and spirit, especially in the church. The desire is there, but often we would rather argue, rant, split, or leave the community of faith than do the hard work of listening to God and to our neighbor to achieve this state. And it takes work to achieve it. Paul goes on to describe it: "Do nothing from selfish ambition or conceit, but in humility regard others as better than yourselves. Let each of you look not to your own interests, but to the interests of others. Let the same mind be in you that was in Christ Jesus" (Philippians 2:3-5). It is a lofty definition of consensus. We often read it as "one mind" and "one accord" but I would suggest that same mind might be different. If we agree that we can live with the decision, isn't our mind the same; haven't we reached one accord?

An Evergreen Story

Evergreen affirmed a basic structure at the Constituting Convention in May 2002. We took that structure to a lawyer and asked for bylaws to be drawn. A meeting was held at Tabernacle Baptist Church in Seattle to read through the bylaws. A diverse group of forty attended the meeting. We began to read through each article

Voices of Evergreen

Rev. Walter Heyman, now pastor of the New Walk Christian Church, had not been active in American Baptist life very long before he was asked to serve as Evergreen's first representative to the ABCUSA General Board. He submitted this testimony in February 2009.

Serving as Evergreen's first General Board Representative to ABCUSA allowed me to experience the operation of other regions and of the broader church community. What I saw was a confirmation of the power and effectiveness of Evergreen's concept that all voices can be heard through use of the caucus model, which creates much more biblical relationships than I have seen in regions that use Robert's Rules of Order, which creates win-lose situations. The struggle for power has caused a lot of division and often made the regions' internal operations ineffective in the mission of Kingdom-building.

The Evergreen model of caucuses creates an equal voice and consensus for decision making, thus allowing relationships to prevail. Finding a common place for us to work eliminates struggles for power and allows us to move forward with the work of God.

Praise be to God, and may the Evergreen Association model be the yeast that changes the ABCUSA into all it can be in Christ Jesus.

and section at a time, asking for comments or concerns after each article. When we got to the final section of Article 4, a disturbed hush, a pregnant silence fell over the room. Article 4 stated: "Manner of Acting: The decisions of the majority of the Voting Delegates shall be the decision or act of the Membership." While no one said anything, an almost audible though unspoken concern seemed to fill the room. After two Biennial meetings of ABC-NW were duly conducted by Robert's Rules of Order and majority rule was followed, people had become leery of "majority rules." Though people voiced concerns, the group knew of no alternatives to Robert's Rules of Order. The suggestion was made that research be done to explore other models of decision making, including consensus.

Mennonite leaders, who had worked with ABC-NW and had used consensus to reach a previous decision, were contacted. I was surprised when the Mennonites, known for doing work by consensus, responded that they did not use consensus in their regular meetings but used Robert's Rules of Order. A Quaker friend of mine shared a concept called "the sense of the meeting," which his Quaker meeting leader would say when they were in agreement. It was similar to consensus but has a much deeper meaning. I was not certain I could adequately convey this concept to our constituency at that time. We found some articles on consensus but nothing very definitive for us. Ultimately, we found few suggestions that held promise for us and decided that the consensus model would be brought forward. We decided to include in the bylaws the practical definition of consensus.

The bylaws read in Article IV Section 5: "The decisions and acts of the membership shall be made by consensus unless noted otherwise. Consensus is a deliberative process where collective decisions are arrived at by a group of individuals working together for the good of the organization and its mission. Conditions under which consensus is formed include open communication in a supportive climate that gives the participants a sense that they have had a fair chance to influence the decision, and that all group members understand and support the decision. Consensus building means that all participants listen carefully and communicate effectively. Consensus has been reached when all parties can at least live with the decision and will agree to support the decision of the body." The last sentence clearly states the basic definition, "all parties can at least live with the decision." This is a bit different from total unison, but perhaps closer to Paul's call to be of the same mind, and being of one accord. After we put consensus in the bylaws as our "manner of acting," the Euro Caucus was still worried. They were concerned that consensus would lead to the tyranny of the one, that one person's disagreement could hijack decisions of the whole group. Despite some lingering concerns, the Euro Caucus agreed to give consensus a try. There is an out in the bylaws, which states that the bylaws can be changed with a three-fourths majority vote. But so far, consensus has worked for us.

How Consensus Works

Evergreen has learned much through the process of consensus building. We quickly learned that you could not just ask a group, "Does everyone agree?" and when no one objected, assume that there was consensus. Likewise, going around a large group and asking for a voice vote one at a time proved to be onerous as well as pressured people to agree with the majority. Though it was our intent to create an environment where all voices felt heard and empowered, we could not naïvely think that the dynamics that exist in the broader society, which marginalizes some groups and empowers others, were left at the door.

We soon discovered that our caucuses could help to build consensus. A smaller group dynamic could serve to more efficiently reach consensus, and account for differences in cultural norms for communicating and decision making. If all caucuses agree, we have consensus. How each caucus achieves consensus is up to the caucus.

One overall frustration for operating under a consensus model is that there are not set rules or "how-to's." Early in the days of Evergreen, Curtis Price, a Euro Caucus leader, said to me after what seemed to him a frustrating meeting, "Where is it written down how to do consensus?" I came back to him and asked, "Are you asking if there are Robert's Rules for Consensus?" He replied, "Well, yes, but I understand, the answer is really no." To be sure, the organic nature of consensus-building work can be disquieting or alarming; it can even feel like total chaos to those who are accustomed to, and therefore more comfortable with, things operating in a so-called "orderly" manner. While Evergreen has grown more comfortable and effective in doing our work by consensus, we are still learning (and unlearning).

Lessons Learned

Despite continued challenges with consensus building, Evergreen has learned some simple but important lessons worth sharing.

Values

Over time we came to the realization that consensus served us because we held the value that every person in the room mattered. We also believed that the people in the room were more important than any decision we were making. If these two core beliefs are not fully embraced, work by consensus is unlikely to be effective.

Being "in full accord and of one mind" as Paul asks the Philippians is by no means easy, as we can attest. Getting to this "one mind" requires, in part, being attuned to God. That is the element our Quaker Friends include in their "sense of the meeting." God's approval is in the group's agreement. In order to fully listen to others in the room, individuals need to let go of what one knows and listen to another's knowledge. One must respect the other more than one wants to reach a decision.

Voices of Evergreen

Barry Briscoe is a layperson who was very involved in Evergreen. His testimony was given in October 2013, the tenth anniversary of our Annual Meetings.

I was elected (ironically by a popular vote) to serve on the transitional executive committee for the newly named Evergreen Association at our Constituting Convention in Tacoma, Washington, in May 2002. This committee comprised two representatives from the African American churches, two from the Asian American churches, and two of us from the European American group, as well as an at-large member. This new association was to be organized by ethnic caucuses. None of us had any idea what difference our diversity could make.

When creating our bylaws, we derived some of our wording about decision making from Robert's Rules of Order, which includes a clause about decision making that says, "Silence will be assumed to mean assent." The pastor of Japanese Baptist spoke up to inform us that this was not a valid assumption in Asian cultures; silence means we haven't talked about it long enough. After significant conversation, the group shifted to decision-making by consensus. We had a lot to learn about the concept of consensus, but we were convinced it was the right direction for us.

I once heard a sermon about how God uses us as his hands and feet to carry out his ministries. Sometimes we don't realize it until we look back.

Too often when we work in the church, the decision becomes more important than God or others in the room. We have had our priorities out of kilter with this kind of thinking. Is the decision more important than the people? Then the decision will get made, but it might happen that people will leave unhappy. I have been in meetings (not Evergreen meetings) where initially the decision was made to do work by consensus, but a proposition was put on the agenda that a minority of people opposed—and opposed enough that consensus would be blocked. The group then said, "Well, we will take a vote," and the majority ruled, but that didn't mean that those opposed felt any better about the issue. In churches when votes happen that are particularly close and the majority celebrates their "win," some of the minority leave the church altogether. Votes too often have winners and losers, and the losers may feel as though they (not just their opinion) are not valued. They leave hoping to find a church where they will be valued.

It cannot be emphasized enough that for consensus to work, all participants must value the people in the room more than the decision being made. If a group can't start there, the group can't really do consensus. It is important that a group leader models these important values. The leader herself must respect each person in the room. The leader must give everyone a chance to be truly heard.

Environment and Group Size

The surroundings in which decisions are made matter. Therefore, the environment of the room requires careful attention. The entire room needs to be well-lit; no one should be in the shadows. If possible, participants should be able to see one another; one circle is preferred. Discourage people from building "second rows." Avoid a sanctuary with bolted-down pews.

Related to overall environment is the issue of the number of people in the room. Maintaining a manageable group size is an important consideration. If the gathering comprises more than twelve people, split the group into two groups so that everyone is in a group of approximately five to twelve individuals.

For very large groups, it is best to have round tables or at least chairs that can be moved into circles so that people can be heard. If this is not done, only a few people will speak, and they will probably speak more than once, even if you have a "rule" that you cannot speak twice until all have spoken at least once. That is why smaller groups are necessary—so that everyone can speak and be heard. Each small group should be given an opportunity to report to the larger group, so that the sense of everyone being heard is maintained. Be sure that a microphone is available so that each group representative can be heard.

Agreeing on Behavior

Early in the life of Evergreen, members of the group read Eric Law's book, *The Wolf Shall Dwell with the Lamb: A Spirituality for Leadership in a Multicultural Community*.[1] Some also attended a session of the Kaleidoscope Institute, and we invited him to lead our leaders' retreat. Eric uses the Respect Communication Guidelines in his work. He encourages leaders to get at least a verbal agreement (if not a signature of participants' agreement) to behave by these guidelines:

R = take RESPONSIBILITY for what you say and feel without blaming others.
E = use EMPATHETIC listening.
S = be SENSITIVE to differences in communication styles.
P = PONDER what you hear and feel before you speak.
E = EXAMINE your own assumptions and perceptions.
C = keep CONFIDENTIALITY.
T = TRUST ambiguity because we are *not* here to debate who is right or wrong.[2]

Taking responsibility for what you say and feel without blaming others means being careful that you are speaking your truth about yourself, not telling others what they should think or do. Using "I" statements is the best practice to live out this guideline. Using "I wonder" and "I noticed" is a great way to abide by this guideline. Using empathetic listening means not just hearing the words but also understanding the speaker's context. When listening well, try to walk in the speaker's shoes.

In the previous chapter, we talked about how some of us are direct communicators and others are indirect. It is important to recognize that all ways of communication are valuable, as are the communicators. Group participants should be sensitive to the fact that others may communicate differently, and they should listen appropriately.

Some of us may speak out before we examine what is prompting us to speak. It helps when a group participant examines his or her motivations before speaking. We may also find that examining our assumptions and perceptions will help us be better group members. Confidentiality should be an agreed-upon behavior. The process of reaching consensus can lead to stories told or words said that should stay in the room. The meeting needs to be a safe place to share viewpoints and concerns that will not be public once the meeting is over. Committing to confidentiality can make the difference between people fully participating or not.

The last guideline is often most troubling: "trust ambiguity because we are *not* here to debate who is right or wrong." We may debate the rightness or wrongness of a decision but that is different than saying that someone is right or wrong. There may be times even in consensus building that you need to hold the trust that God is in room and will help us in our decision making if we trust one another.

Leaders are not limited to these specific guidelines. Groups may develop their own expectations. However and whatever the group decides, it is important for good group decision making to develop agreed-upon guidelines and standards of behavior.

Time

One of the first concerns raised about consensus is that it takes more time. The answer is yes, it often does. But the time is worth taking because the end result will be owned by the group. The more important the decision is to the group, the more this will be true. Because the group has taken the time to listen to everyone's concerns, in the end all will affirm and own the decision. We have found that the benefits outweigh the extra time.

In recent years, I have begun conducting a workshop with a Quaker friend in which she emphasizes that one must not allow time to dictate when the decision has to be made. She tells the story of her local meeting deciding to get new chairs and then taking three years to choose which chairs to buy. Their Quaker visitors today will almost always say, "What wonderful chairs you have!"

In some instances there may be legitimate time constraints for making a decision. If, for example, a tree fell onto the roof of the church and damaged it, the decision is more urgent and the agreement is to ask a person or small group to take care of the problem for the larger group. However, with a few exceptions, it is important to refrain from demanding that decisions are made in a short time frame, because it is possible that certain people will feel coerced into the decision. It may seem subtle, but not allowing time for decisions to be made means that the decision itself has more value. It is easier to give people space to make decisions than it is to help all the people in the room understand a decision they did not have enough space to consider. I was recently part of a group that covenanted to make decisions by consensus. On the day we were to make our biggest decision, we began our work at 8:00 a.m. At 10:30 p.m. one person was blocking the decision. That person was me. People had to leave at 3:30 a.m., the next morning, to catch planes home. The perception was that we didn't have time to put the decision aside for further consideration, and eventually I agreed not to block consensus. I felt coerced by time if not by the group. I still believe that if we had not felt constrained by time, the decision would have been different.

Role of the Facilitator

The facilitator (leader) of a group trying to reach consensus is a lot more powerful than the leader of a group using Robert's Rules of

Order. Robert's Rules of Order has established rules for how decisions will be made. In contrast, with consensus, there are no set rules about how decisions are to be reached other than that decisions will be made by consensus. It can be easy to lose control of the room if people start talking over each other or raising their voices because they have forgotten the communication guidelines they agreed on earlier. On the other hand, it is easy to intentionally or unintentionally shut someone down because the leader does have control of who will be recognized to speak. Establishing guidelines at the beginning of the meeting provides ways to monitor behavior if it becomes necessary, so control is less of an issue. The facilitator must continue to keep the guidelines in mind and help the group return to them. He or she must remember that everyone in the room matters, that the people in the room are more important than the agenda.

Sometimes the facilitator may be too close to the issue and therefore needs to step back. If the issue is one in which the facilitator has a stake, I would suggest that an outside facilitator be identified. Such a facilitator can more easily manage the discussion and see possibilities for consensus than someone who may have opinions on the matter at hand.

Tools for Building Consensus

Because ensuring that every voice is heard is vital to the consensus-building process, we have created some tools that can be used to hear all voices. We have already talked about breaking larger groups into smaller ones. What follows are other tools that can be used to attain the goal of hearing everyone.

Talking stick. This is a tool we use to be sure everyone has a chance to speak. The only person allowed to speak is the one who holds the "talking stick." It assures that the person speaking won't be interrupted.[3] We tend to use the Mutual Invitation described next instead of worrying about having enough talking sticks for every group that may meet. As a symbol that our leadership understands our commitment to hearing all voices, we have over time given talking sticks to our chairpersons, both as they come in and as they leave, to thank them for their service.

Mutual Invitation. Another tool we've found helpful for ensuring that all voices are heard is "mutual invitation." Eric Law explains Mutual Invitation this way:

> The leader or a designated person will share first. After that person has spoken, he or she then invites another to share. Who you invite does not need to be the person next to you. After the next person has spoken, that person is given the privilege to invite another to share. If you don't want to say anything, simply say "pass" and proceed to invite another. . . . Do this until everyone has been invited. We invite you to listen and not respond to someone's sharing immediately. There will be time to respond and ask clarifying questions after everyone has had opportunity to share.[4]

Mutual invitation provides everyone the opportunity to have a say before the group moves into more general discussion. Each person gets to speak before anyone else can speak again. This process honors an individual's decision to participate or not. When working on decision making, it is helpful to go around and get opinions from everyone before opening a more general discussion. Toward the end, go back to mutual invitation to determine if everyone is in agreement. Mutual invitation forces people to listen to others because invitations are extended in no particular order.

This tool can sometimes help even when the group has time constraints. I have found that if people are aware of time constraints with the group, they will self-regulate how long they talk. I use this when we are in a general discussion, but it can be used even when in a decision-making process. I will say, "Because we have ten minutes to work on this issue, I'm going to ask that, in our first go-round by mutual invitation, we be aware of the time." This will encourage everyone to limit their sharing so that everyone has an opportunity to share. Every now and then I might have to remind people of time constraints, but I have always done it gently and as nonjudgmentally as possible.

Often people might need to be reminded when using this tool to invite the next person to speak. The advantage of this, though, is that it gives the floor to people for a short period of time, and they indicate that they are finished by inviting the next person to speak. This helps those who tend to interrupt and gives everyone a chance to speak.

Straw Poll. Another useful tool is to take a "straw poll" at some point in the discussion. It might be at the very beginning to see if most people are already in agreement, or part-way through to get a feel of where people are at that point. Of course a straw poll can be taken at the end to double check to make sure that people are in agreement. I have seen significant shifts when using this tool, from almost no agreement to complete consensus.

An extension of the straw poll is to ask people how much, on a scale of one to five, they are in agreement. One is total agreement; two, agreement with some reservations; three, agreement with serious reservations; four, blocking agreement; and five, serious questions before they can move ahead. If the poll reveals mostly ones and twos, the group may be able to move ahead if the concerns of the twos can easily be addressed. If there are threes, you need to find out their reservations; and if possible address those, then perhaps consensus can be found. If there are fours, stop and find what can be done to address their concerns. Of course, for fives, the questions need to be answered. Everyone needs to be at ones and twos in order to move forward. It goes something like this:

> In full agreement with the decision, hold up one finger. Not in full agreement, but are happy to support it, hold up two fingers. Serious doubts about the decision but are willing to support it, hold up three fingers. Serious concerns about the decision, hold up four fingers. Cannot support the decision and are ready to block it, hold up five fingers. Some folks add: serious questions, but if these questions can be answered and you might be persuaded to move forward, hold up six fingers.

By using such a straw poll, it is possible to get a read of the room. The leader can identify the people who are having difficulty and get their concerns out on the table to give focus to the discussion and perhaps move toward something upon which everyone can agree.

Consensus Put to the Test

Our determination to use consensus was tested in the beginning of Evergreen. One of our first tasks was to decide how to recognize ordinations. It was decided by a diverse group to establish a Ministerial Standards and Concerns Committee with appropriate guidelines for how caucuses would appoint representatives to the committee, and to follow the guidelines recommended by ABCUSA. As executive minister, I wanted to be clear what the Association would be doing by adopting these procedures. Ordination of homosexuals in the church was, after all, the crux of the matter in the separation from ABC-NW. Our challenge was to build consensus around this issue.

The proposal put to Evergreen was to adopt the "Recommended Procedures of American Baptist Churches," which do not say anything about sexual orientation. The procedures as outlined made several requirements of candidates for ordination including education, a recommendation from one's local church, signing the

American Baptist Churches Minister's Code of Ethics (see appendix), and a call to a ministry. The procedures say nothing about sexual orientation. Therefore, we proposed that sexual orientation would not be an issue for any Evergreen candidate who met these identified criteria.

Some individuals in the African American Caucus had problems with Evergreen remaining silent on the issue. In fact, the chair of Evergreen was one of the most vocal in expressing his discomfort. The Black Caucus had several meetings to try to come to consensus about whether they would agree to the procedures. The result was that they weren't in agreement about what to do. There were some in the Caucus who wanted to take a stand against the ordination of people who were LGBTQ, but the Caucus never reached any consensus on the matter. Eventually, the person with the most concerns resigned. That is the only time we have experienced someone leaving due to our use of consensus.

Another instance where consensus was tested occurred around the development of a statement on Sacred Action Against Racism, which was presented by a member of the Black Caucus at a 2009 Annual Meeting. The Black Caucus had some conversation about the statement and thought it ought to go to the entire body.

Because there was only one copy of the statement document, the call to Sacred Action Against Racism was read out loud by Ken Curl, who happened to be the incoming chair from the Black Caucus. He assumed that everyone was in agreement., but others said that no consensus had been established. Ken then asked for a standing affirmation, and after most people stood, he once again affirmed the statement.

At the next executive committee meeting, we talked about how this process was not in keeping with the consensus-building model we had developed. We discussed the fact that, because we had had only one copy of the statement, many were uncomfortable with affirming something they couldn't read for themselves. The executive committee recommended to the Association board that a committee of at least three people (one from each Caucus) be assigned to follow through on the statement. After several meetings the committee of three—Yosh Nakagawa from the Asian Caucus, Tom Nielsen from the Euro Caucus, and Ken Curl from the Black Caucus—developed the following recommendations for each Caucus: (1) name one person to a strategic action coordinating team tasked with meeting regularly to respond to injustices as they arise; (2) find Caucus members to participate in a year-long covenant group to share stories and pray about justice issues; and (3) find one Caucus member to serve on a team on justice issues and immigration issues.

Sadly, we did not follow through on the specific proposals, though the Sacred Action Team decided to hold some "Sacred Conversations." Although our work in sacred conversations is not about reaching consensus, it does help us in community to practice the listening and love that will help us achieve one accord. We used several processes in our sacred conversation; some have been hosted in individuals' homes, with small groups of people attending. Others have been held in conjunction with our annual meetings. These sacred conversations use a few different processes. Several used an article, book, or video, and asks the group (or groups) to respond beginning with the words "I noticed" or "I wonder." Others used a process called "photo-language" from the Kaleidoscope Institute. In this process participants view an array of photos and are asked to select a photo that answers for them the question put forward.

Year to year our conversations have always been poignant and challenging. In 2016 we used a slightly different model. Our Sacred Conversation was on gun violence, and we used excerpts from President George W. Bush's and President Barack Obama's remarks at a Dallas police officer's memorial service. We had three rounds of questions that the small groups were to answer. The last round asked, "What is God asking you to do, be, or change as a result of this conversation?"

Unintended Consequences

As with any organization, doing work a new way brings unintended consequences. An unintended consequence of Evergreen deciding to work by consensus is that churches are considering the consensus model for themselves. In fact, Wedgwood Community Church, a Euro American congregation in Seattle, has decided to make all of its decisions by consensus. Many of their laity, as well as their pastor, were active in forming Evergreen. While streamlining their organizational structure, Wedgewood decided they liked how Evergreen operates and adopted our way of doing business as a local church. So far, it is working well.

Other leaders have taken Mutual Invitation and consensus decision making to their committee or group meetings in their churches. They report better meetings and more satisfaction in giving leadership in those meetings.

Questions for Reflection

1. What do you value most when working in a group?
2. How do you know you've been heard in a group setting?
3. Have you ever done work by consensus? If so, describe the group and your feelings about the work you did.
4. How does consensus help a group do its work?
5. How does consensus hinder a group from doing its work?
6. How does one help members of a group listen to each other?
7. How can you use the tools of Mutual Invitation and RESPECT Communication Guidelines with your groups?
8. What questions would you address in a Sacred Conversation?

Voices of Evergreen

Rev. James T. Winbush, a member of the Black Caucus, was a son-in-the-ministry of Rev. Dr. Leon Jones, pastor emeritus of Martin Luther King Jr. Memorial Baptist Church. James served as chair of the ABC-NW Task Force for the New Region. In July 2008 he gave this testimony.

Take a spiritual walk with me for just a moment. Close your eyes and picture your church or local association. How often have you had the opportunity to fellowship or worship with your brothers or sisters in Christ of another culture or race? Where can you experience this in the body of Christ? Where among the body of believers is there opportunity to witness a baptism performed in Japanese, or participate as African Americans serve a southern barbecue meal to Asians, or enjoy the freedom to express your likes and dislikes in an open forum and come away assured that you were heard? It must be Evergreen.

The Evergreen Association of American Baptist Churches is a place where people of color are no longer just informed of what's happening in their association by Euro Americans. Evergreen is an association where people of color are providing leadership and formulating policies in partnership with our Euro American sisters and brothers. Evergreen is where collaborative ministries are an objective, not just talking points. Evergreen is not your standard association of tradition, but it could become the standard for the future.

CHAPTER 4

Cultural Sensitivity

> In that renewal there is no longer Greek and Jew, circumcised and uncircumcised, barbarian, Scythian, slave and free; but Christ is all and in all!
>
> As God's chosen ones, holy and beloved, clothe yourselves with compassion, kindness, humility, meekness, and patience. Bear with one another and, if anyone has a complaint against another, forgive each other; just as the Lord has forgiven you, so you also must forgive. Above all, clothe yourselves with love, which binds everything together in perfect harmony. And let the peace of Christ rule in your hearts, to which indeed you were called in the one body. And be thankful. Let the word of Christ dwell in you richly; teach and admonish one another in all wisdom; and with gratitude in your hearts sing psalms, hymns, and spiritual songs to God. And whatever you do, in word or deed, do everything in the name of the Lord Jesus, giving thanks to God the Father through him. (Colossians 3:11-17)

Paul on the one hand paints a picture of equality in his letter to the Colossians, calling them to inclusive ministry, reminding them that in the eyes of God we are all loved and we should do likewise. It can be confusing when I also say that this passage acknowledges our differences and we are at our best when we join together with our differences, not trying to leave our differences at the door. Although we are all loved by God we are loved in our uniquenesses and we bring our identities (our cultures, our gender identity, our traditions) to God's table. Working with others who are different, united in Christ, makes us powerful.

Working as an inclusive organization has been a joy. As seen in the testimonies throughout this volume, all of us at Evergreen have experienced a great deal of personal and collective growth as a result of this process. The experience has not been without its trials, however. Just as the early church had its ups and downs, its understandings and misunderstandings, so have we. Much of our misunderstanding has been related to figuring out how to work together in ways that take into account our cultural differences.

One model of inclusive understanding that has helped me lead this effort is the Developmental Model of Intercultural Sensitivity put forward by Milton J. Bennett and Janet M. Bennett in the 1990s, during the Summer Institute of Intercultural Communication (SIIC) held at Reed College in Portland, Oregon.[1] The Bennetts' work in intercultural communications, which has been useful in education, government, and industry, has also proved helpful in our inclusive ministry work.

The Developmental Model of Intercultural Sensitivity (DMIS) (found on page 56) represents a continuum. On one end of the continuum is a monocultural mindset (the belief that there is only one culture or that one culture is better than another); the other end is a multicultural mindset (a belief that embraces cultural differences). The model is developmental in approach because it assumes an individual's ability to move from a monocultural to multicultural mindset through education and other experiences.

On the far left of the monocultural mindset is **denial.** Those in denial do not understand that different cultures exist. This may happen because they are isolated in a homogeneous group and have not had the opportunity to experience cultural difference or because they intentionally separate themselves from all others. They might expect that McDonald's serves the same menu around the world. People in denial are not prepared to accept differences, even those obvious cultural differences that can be experienced with the five senses.

To the right of denial on the DMIS continuum is **defense.** A person with this mindset does not deny the existence of other cultures, yet he or she believes his or her culture is far superior to others. There is an ironic twist to this mindset. Those who have spent some time in another culture, such as exchange students or missionaries, may grow to think their home culture does not stand up to that of the country they visited. In their minds, the visited country's culture is far superior to others, including theirs. They believe if the home culture would just do things like the country they visited, then all would be well with the world.

From this defense mindset, people may move into a mindset known as **minimization.** In this phase there is some recognition of other cultures, but all cultures are understood to be alike at the core. People in this mindset might use phrases such as "color blind" and "we are really all alike." Although they acknowledge the many different cultures, this mindset fails to recognize the particularities of the cultures.

On the multicultural side of the DMIS continuum, there is first a mindset of **acceptance,** an awareness of other cultures and their significant differences from one another. The downside of this mindset is that people may accept behaviors, values, and traditions that they otherwise might not, reasoning that these differences are simply cultural.

As one develops along the continuum, the next move is to a mindset of **adaptation.** In this phase, people are effective at being able to understand and be understood across cultural boundaries.

They begin to make a seamless transition among cultures, with deep understanding of nuance.

On the far right of the continuum is **integration.** Perhaps the best example of someone who has moved along the continuum to integration is someone who understands another culture's humor.

When seeking to grow in cultural understanding, individuals may take steps for themselves to produce movement along the continuum. Thus, along with describing the phases, the DMIS also unpacks tasks one might do to move from one place on the continuum to the next. For example, a person moving from denial might be given opportunities to experience another culture and see that other cultures exist. In some communities, this may be as simple as going to a grocery store and seeing the different aisles of Asian or Hispanic foods. It may be a mission fair where the native dress and foods of people from different countries are shared. Eventually, people would understand that there are other cultures outside their own.

Those in the defense mindset may be helped by seeing what different cultures have in common. For instance, all cultures have basic needs such as food and shelter. This group may resist but nonetheless must be given the experiences necessary to see that others are not a threat to their lifestyle or culture.

Perhaps the hardest to understand and begin to move forward are those stuck in the minimization or "color blind" mindset. With this mindset, one must do the exact opposite of what one does to move out of defense. Those with a minimization mindset should be encouraged to better understand and appreciate the uniqueness of their own culture.

THE DEVELOPMENTAL MODEL OF INTERCULTURAL SENSITIVITY

ETHNOCENTRIC STAGES MONOCULTURAL MINDSET			ETHNORELATIVE STAGES MULTICULTURAL MINDSET		
Denial of Difference	**Defense Against Difference**	**Minimization of Difference**	**Acceptance of Difference**	**Adaption to Difference**	**Integration of Difference**
DEFINITION					
Inability to construe cultural difference, indicated by benign stereotyping and superficial statements of tolerance.	Recognition of cultural difference coupled with negative evaluation of most variations from native culture—the greater the difference, the more negative the evaluation. Characterized by dualistic us/them thinking and frequently accompanied by overt negative stereotyping.	Recognition and acceptance of superficial cultural differences such as eating customs, etc., while holding that all human beings are essentially the same.	Recognition and appreciation of cultural differences in behavior and values.	The development of communication skills that enable intercultural communication. Effective use of empathy, or frame-of-reference shifting, to understand and be understood across cultural boundaries.	The internalization of bicultural or multicultural frames of reference. Maintaining a definition of identity that is "marginal" to any particular culture. Seeing one's self as "in process."
DEVELOPMENTAL TASK					
To recognize the existence of cultural differences	Mitigate polarization by emphasizing "common humanity"	Develop cultural self-awareness	Refine analysis of cultural contrasts	Develop frame-of-reference-shifting skills	Resolve the multicultural identity

Material taken from handout copyrighted from Janet Bennett, 2004, and derived from: Bennett, Milton J. "Towards Ethnorelativism: A Developmental Model of Intercultural Sensitivity," In Education for the Intercultural Experience. 2n ed., edited by R. Michael Paige, Yarmouth, ME: Intercultural Press, 1993. Bennett, Janet M. "Cultural Marginality: Identity Issues in Intercultural Training," In Education for the Intercultural Experience. 2n ed., edited by R. Michael Paige, Yarmouth, ME: Intercultural Press, 1993. Bennett, Janet M., & Milton J. Bennett. "Developing Intercultural Sensitivity: An Integrative Approach to Global and Domestic Diversity." In Handbook of Intercultural Training. 3rd ed., edited by D. Landis, J.M. Bennett, & M.J. Bennett, Thousand Oaks, CA: Sage, 2004.

Evergreen's Mindset

Even after Evergreen had begun the work of becoming intentionally inclusive, we were surprised to find that most of our folk had a minimization mindset, believing that the best way to deal with differences is not to focus on them. At a leadership team retreat, we took an inventory (Intercultural Development Inventory by Richard Hammer) that measures intercultural sensitivity. Since we had already been working together across cultural lines, we assumed we would score in the acceptance range of the continuum. Instead, as a group we had a minimization mindset. We recognized differences but too often minimized them. We were doing our work in ways that kept us unaware of those differences. We then tasked our caucuses to first understand themselves better. DMIS theory teaches us that understanding our own cultural values and traditions would help move the group into a more multicultural mindset.

A minimization mindset has been present throughout our history. Since the inception of the Evergreen "experiment," we have sought to do the work of our organization through caucuses, made up of different ethnic groups. During the very early years of Evergreen, the caucus system was challenged. Someone, often a white male, would ask, "Why do we have these different caucuses? Isn't the idea to be one? How can we be one if we all meet in separate groups?" The different caucuses put our differences on display, which caused discomfort for those who sought to work inclusively by minimizing cultural difference. That the question was asked largely by whites led me to ponder the connection between minimization and white privilege.

As our work continued, I assumed that the value and necessity of caucus work would prove apparent and that the minimization mindset would have been minimized. Yet, as we approached our tenth anniversary, hints of minimization surfaced with respect to our Hispanic Caucus. In early March 2012, the executive committee was asked and approved the idea of adding an Hispanic member to the executive committee. We had one church and a small group of folks in Evergreen who spoke Spanish and/or are Hispanic. We anticipated growth of this caucus. However, our bylaws required there to be at least two churches to establish a caucus. Thus the addition of an Hispanic committee member was challenged on the grounds that a one-church Hispanic Caucus represented a departure from the Association's bylaws.

While the caucuses ultimately decided in favor of adding an Hispanic executive committee member, the discussion about the legitimacy proved hurtful to the two Hispanic Caucus members present. One member later wrote to me: "I was very hurt by the comments on the 'non-existence' of the Hispanic Caucus, because it made us invisible once again. This is precisely the issue that we as Hispanics—and I am sure that other ethnicities too—have experienced again and again. We are not a 'prophecy,' in fact we are the present reality of this Association and of the country as a whole."

This member further stated that the bylaws requiring at least two churches for a caucus to be seated did not acknowledge the reality that there were Hispanics in the Association whose interests would not be fully represented by a Euro Caucus. The Hispanic members initially declined the invitation for one Hispanic to join the executive committee but after a conversation with Yosh sent a representative to the executive committee and became a contributing caucus to Evergreen. The work to ensure that we challenge our own thinking about how to work effectively across cultures is ongoing. Despite our best efforts, we can never believe we have fully arrived.

In the early days of Evergreen, our commitment to caucuses was tested. At our very first Annual Meeting, the Black Caucus in their meeting decided that their representative, Rev. James Winbush, could no longer represent them because he had left the Evergreen

Voices of Evergreen

Rev. M. Christopher Boyer, who came to Good Shepherd Baptist Church, having spent most of his ministry in the theatre arts field, is a pastor who has a unique relationship with Evergreen. He shared this reflection in August 2016.

Those of you who know me know that I am very rarely at a loss for words. So it might surprise you to know that it's difficult for me to say what Evergreen means to me—not because Evergreen is not important in my life but because it has become so important.

I am a "recovering" Southern Baptist. While I was in college, the fundamentalists began their takeover of the Convention's structure. By the time I was a seminary student, the "truth squads" were out in full force, hunting for heretics and noncompliant congregations to eject. A long twenty years later, I found in Evergreen a group of churches and individuals that had managed to retain their integrity and their connection to a national Baptist body. Evergreen helped heal my deepest wounds and gave me hope for the future of the Baptist Movement.

Evergreen has been very important to me as a Southern white man. My heritage is inescapable. Some of my ancestors were slaveholders, and I am still working to be free of the blinders of white privilege and misogyny. My brothers and sisters from all the Evergreen caucuses have been patient and loving, helping me see new points of view and gently correcting my most egregious errors and assumptions. I am overwhelmed by the kindness and compassion as they have revealed Christ to me over the years.

church, where he had been a member, and had not yet joined another church. The Black Caucus determined that he had to be replaced. They selected from their membership an associate minister from Tabernacle Missionary Baptist Church, Kelly Coleman, naming him as chair.

After the meeting, a Euro American came to me and stated that the Black Caucus couldn't do that. The whole body had affirmed James Winbush, and the Black Caucus couldn't change it. But I knew that, for whatever reason the Black Caucus had determined to make the change, it was a test to see if Evergreen was serious about the responsibilities of the caucuses. In the end, the associational body accepted their announcement and moved on. It wasn't the only time the Black Caucus acted with such autonomy. Just a few months later, they had reason again to name another replacement among their associational representation. And the Association again tacitly affirmed their autonomous right to choose.

I am convinced that if the larger body had in some way challenged the Black Caucus action at the first annual meeting or at the later meeting in April, we would not have as active a constituency among the African Americans as we do today. I'm not saying it was an intentional test of power, but it functioned as such. If Evergreen had failed them at that point, Evergreen would not look like it does today. No one anticipated the action, but it was pivotal in assuring the non-European caucuses in particular that the power thought to be in their hands really was theirs to exercise.

Questions for Reflection

1. Where are you on the Developmental Model of Intercultural Sensitivity (DMIS) continuum?
2. What insights does identifying your mindset offer to you?
3. What might you do as an individual to be more sensitive in a multicultural setting?

Voices of Evergreen

Angela Farrar (Small) is a member of the Black Caucus. She had been pastor of First Baptist Church of Mountlake Terrace (a Euro American congregation) and served for a short time as Evergreen's Associate for Youth Ministry. In April 2008 she shared her testimony.

Ten years ago, as a seminary student having sensed God's call to serve in ordained ministry, I started to attend Region meetings at the encouragement of my student mentor, Dr. Paul Aita. My first reaction to the experience was mixed: meeting people was wonderful, but the business side of things felt lifeless. First, I never got Robert's Rules of Order, and probably never will! Also, nothing we talked about, or how we talked about them, reflected the passion for ministry that I heard when talking one-on-one with the laity and clergy whom I met. I often left thinking, "God could not have called me to this."

Since then I've happily served the Association in various roles and committees. What changed? Not using Robert's Rules of Order freed us to use consensus building. Also, seeing how we have learned and grown through the genuine cultural inclusion of the caucus system has been an awakening. The caucuses give room for more participation from more people. Participation also improves by communication style; introverts get more voice and so do nonlinear thinkers. *The Body of Christ in all its diverse giftedness has better expression in this new way of being an association of churches*. In short, I see the caucus system and consensus decision making reflecting God's love and interest in each person and each group, so that true community results. Did God call me to this? Yes! Amen!

CHAPTER 5

It's All about Relationships

> Then some people came, bringing to him a paralyzed man, carried by four of them. And when they could not bring him to Jesus because of the crowd, they removed the roof above him; and after having dug through it, they let down the mat on which the paralytic lay. When Jesus saw their faith, he said to the paralytic, "Son, your sins are forgiven." (Mark 2:3-5)

The story of friends bringing a paralyzed man to Jesus is told in Matthew and Luke as well as Mark. In all three narratives it says, "When Jesus saw *their* faith." It is all about relationships. It was not the paralytic's faith, but that of his friends, that moved Jesus to healing! It is in our relationships that God can add blessing. We are not physically paralyzed, but we can be individually and organizationally paralyzed in other ways. Our relationships are a gift from God, and God both blesses them and expects us to put them to use (as God expects us to put all our gifts to work). The illustration of the friends of the paralytic and the demonstration of their faith is an illustration to us of the strength of relationships.

Evergreen places value on relationships and providing a sense of belonging. We believe we have done our best work when we include people from all the caucuses, and from laity as well as clergy. The decision to govern by caucus has proven a powerful vehicle for expressing how valuable relationships and belonging are. The testimonies of folks active in Evergreen, featured throughout this book, are a testament to our successfully embracing and fulfilling our commitment to our deeply held values. This chapter will define our organizational structure and explain how it has reinforced relationships and belonging in Evergreen.

Organization by ethnic caucuses is a foundation of Evergreen Association. This means that instead of being organized along geographical lines, we are organized by ethnic caucuses. Evergreen bylaws require that all caucuses have a national American Baptist Churches USA caucus or alliance to which it can relate (except for the Euro American Caucus because there isn't one nationally).[1] At Evergreen's founding, the Black, Asian, and Euro caucuses were all we had. The Hispanic caucus was added later.

In Evergreen, the caucuses were initially developed based on the racial makeup of congregations, which proved a challenge for some congregations where the pastor and the congregation differed ethnically. The practice evolved to allowing individuals to make choices to attend the caucus where they best identified or understood their role. That meant a congregation could have their pastor in one caucus while members attended another; or as in the case of the Asian caucus, having members or pastors of an Asian congregation attending the Asian caucus instead of the Euro-Caucus.

Caucuses work for us. They represent an acknowledgment and embrace of diversity, thereby providing a sense of belonging among the various constituents the caucuses represent. Caucuses also allow a safe place for dialogue, difference, and agreement. If the caucus's agreement is seen differently by other caucuses, there is safety in the caucus, and individuals do not feel they are standing alone. The following is an example of an occasion where the caucus system helped achieve an end that would likely not have been achieved in the broader group.

An Evergreen Story

The caucuses had received a report of what their churches had given to mission and support of American Baptist Churches USA. For the Black Caucus, the amounts were zero across the board. In their caucus meeting, they had the opportunity to discuss among themselves what this meant. The leaders agreed that they weren't holding up their part of the responsibility in Evergreen, and they determined to do something about it. They reported such to the rest of the Association when the larger group reconvened.

Later, I checked in with Black Caucus members. They said that if the materials had been handed out in the larger group meeting, not only would they not have had the discussion and decided to take action to step up; they would have defended why they *didn't* give anything to American Baptist Mission.

The Value of Feeling Valued

The establishment of caucuses signal that Evergreen want everyone to know they are valued. The result has been that people own the decisions and work of the Association and are more inclined to participate in it.

This value of being valued is reflected in other specific provisions that were included in Evergreen bylaws to ensure the caucus structure's success. First, we do not require a quorum of a specific number but rather that at least one representative from each caucus be present for us to do business. No business can occur useless everyone is at the table. Every group is valued; each group has a voice. Second, our bylaws require that the chair and other officers rotate among the caucuses. This allows each caucus an opportunity to have representation among the leadership. Third, our structure does not call for a nominating committee. Instead, each caucus develops its own unique process for determining leadership.

Consensus building has as a goal that every voice be heard. Large groups can hinder this goal. When decisions are made in Evergreen, consensus building begins at the caucus level. The caucuses provide built-in smaller groups (some of which are subdivided) where voices can be heard and unity achieved. While consensus-building can feel messy in the midst of the process, if followed through to the end, decisions tend to be better embraced by all.

When power is distributed in a way that everyone feels a part, everyone is more likely to own the outcome. This solidifies the feeling that Evergreen really does belong to us all.

An Evergreen Story

An illustration of how our caucus creates a sense of inclusion happened in 2016 when Evergreen went through the process of forming the search committee for a new executive minister. According to our bylaws, each caucus must select two representatives to serve on the search committee. When we were putting together a search committee in October 2016, the first group of representatives selected by the caucuses was criticized by the body-at-large as lacking gender and age diversity. Each caucus met again to determine if caucus members were willing to make adjustments to address those issues. Some were; some were not. The Evergreen Way required us to defer to the caucus group's decision; our consensus starts with our caucuses.

When tasks that require special skill sets are to be completed, the Evergreen Way still requires us to honor our commitment to diversity. For example, in 2016 we brought together a data-gathering design team to determine how to collect feedback from the Evergreen family about the effectiveness of our work. Although the caucuses did not name the team, the people recruited from different caucuses had some skills that would help the team achieve its goal.

Voices of Evergreen

Rev. Sarah Halverson-Cano serves as pastor at Fairview Community Church in Costa Mesa, Orange County, California, which is a congregation now dually aligned with the American Baptist Churches USA and the United Church of Christ. Rev. Halverson-Cano is ordained in the United Church of Christ and is a Euro-Caucus member.

It was my third year in attendance at our annual regional meeting of the Evergreen Association of American Baptist Churches, and I finally felt like I had friends there. What a feeling it is to belong! It's wonderful to feel like I am a part of the Region—

Intentional inclusion was achieved with the knowledge that each caucus has within it the skill set necessary to accomplish any task.

An Evergreen Story

Rev. Beverly Spears, a former Catholic, received her seminary training at a Jesuit school and was ordained by University Baptist Church, a primarily Euro congregation, to serve in ecumenical ministry. A member of the Black Caucus, she served as a part-time ministry associate for development for Evergreen, She gave this testimony in October 2008.

> I could answer the question "What's so special about Evergreen?" by saying that we are unique among regional Baptist bodies because of our ethnic caucus governing structure and our practice of consensus model decision making. I could answer that question simply by saying how ethnically and culturally diverse our member churches are,

even though I'm from a different denomination, and even though we're so far away. There's a place for me in Evergreen, and there's a place for Fairview Church.

Being a part of Evergreen for the past three years has made me wonder how difficult (or easy) it is for people to feel like they belong in our church communities. In fact, studies show that unless visitors meet and bond with seven people—despite their relationship with a pastor, the quality of the sermons, and the mission of the church—they will end up falling by the wayside and leaving. I came away from the annual regional meeting thinking again how happy I am to be in the Evergreen region.

and how we value that diversity. While all that is true, it doesn't begin to tell the whole story of what is special about Evergreen.

The deeper story of its uniqueness is about the challenges as well as the opportunities that our ethnic caucus system and our way of decision making bring. It is about how tedious and sometimes frustrating working toward consensus can be, but how deeply satisfying it is to know that all voices have been heard and valued in coming to decisions.

The deeper story is about the courage of the members of the Euro Caucus as they have grappled with how to be in right relationship with themselves and others when they no longer function as the dominant culture in an organization. It is about the determination and commitment of the Black Caucus to find ways of helping member black churches with low or no participation to be more comfortable and involved in Evergreen. The story is about how the Asian

Voices of Evergreen

The first time Ken Curl came to an Evergreen Association board meeting, he was elected to the executive committee to fulfill the partial term of our previous chair. He stayed on for two additional years as the Black Caucus representative. Then he became vice-chair and subsequently served as chair again. He gave his testimony in August 2008.

Christians all over the world know that God is love, and yet as human beings we don't always show our love for one another. The Evergreen Association of American Baptist Churches is based on the principle of love. We love one another, and we are not afraid to show it. We show it through the respect we have for one another's opinions. We show it through making decisions by consensus, through entering into common ministry, and through our common goal of sharing the Good News with a hurting world. We have broken down barriers that normally separate us, such as race, sexual orientation, and socioeconomic class. We dispel the notion that, as Dr. Martin Luther King Jr. decried, 11:00 a.m. Sunday morning has to be the most segregated hour in America.

When I began my journey with Evergreen, it was because my pastor asked me to become involved, but that's not what has kept me involved. What has kept me involved is the love that I feel every time I attend an Evergreen function. Evergreen knows that the heart of God is love.

Caucus reaches far beyond Evergreen into a national network of Asian caucuses, and of its efforts to recognize and include Hispanic and Native American churches in the work of the Association.

The deeper story is that Evergreen leadership is constantly involved in cultural competency training so they can in turn bring this training to churches. The deeper story is that balancing power and taking the time to make sound, prayerful decisions is hard work. The fact is that being in relationship with one another as individuals, churches, and associations is hard work, and that valuing and respecting our differences is deeply prayerful work.

What's so special about Evergreen? This organization walks the talk of love, inclusion, and empowerment. We truly love God, and in the name of Jesus we strive to love and value one another.

An Evergreen Story

In June 2009 Curtis Price was asked to share a witness. Curtis had been on the Vision Committee and became the first Euro Caucus person to serve as chair of Evergreen Association. He had no idea when he said yes to that position that Yosh Nakagawa would almost haunt him, "watching him like a hawk" to be sure he didn't resort to a typical European manner of abusing power in contradiction to the Evergreen Way. This is how Curtis tells the story:

> My wife, Robbin, and I got a fire pit for our porch last year, and with the warmth finally arriving, it has been perfect for enjoying evenings on the deck, roasting marshmallows and relaxing by the fire. After building a fire the other night, I noticed that the wood I was using flamed up very quickly, got very bright, and then burned up fast. Soon I had to pick up another log and throw it on. However, this one was a hardwood that burned very differently. It didn't make big flames, and it burned very slowly yet produced -a lot of heat.

I marveled at the difference between the two and the kind of fire each produced. The first log was much more exciting to watch, and it certainly was easier to get going. But the second log lasted and was able to produce more warmth for a longer time. So it is with a ministry such as the one we have in Evergreen. In our time together, we have witnessed many events and ideas that quickly ignited our passions and burned brightly for a while. They were inspiring and exciting, yet that excitement was difficult to maintain and the passion quickly waned. The meatier core values that guide who we are as a community of churches, which can be much less exciting, last and produce the real heat.

In my time with Evergreen, I have often been on a quest for the big idea that would ignite people's passions and draw them into relationship with this wonderful organization. But more and more I am realizing that what truly

Voices of Evergreen

One of the treasures of Evergreen was the calling of "Clem" Winbush, an African American woman, to be the executive assistant and minister of mission support. Clem has supported me in a number of ways (and makes me look good); we enjoy our partnership in ministry. Here is her testimony.

Do you know what it's like to be in the exact place that God has for you at a given time? Evergreen is such a place for me.

Being here is God's divine answer to my prayer, "What do you have for me to do, Lord? What's the next step in my life?" From the initial job posting, through the get-acquainted exercise formally called an interview, to the changing position description inspires commitment is the solid foundational ideals and concepts that take time to convey and understand. It is our commitment to equitable community, our focus on relationship and trust, and our common desire to see each other produce good fruit that will hold us together.

Consensus, the Caucuses, the Respect Guidelines—all of these are tools we use to lift up these ideals, but it is the ideals themselves that are compelling and have to be experienced to really grasp them. We have struggled to find easy ways to tell our story over the years, and the truth is that any attempt to covey who we are in a short document or presentation will always pale in comparison to immersion in the culture of Evergreen. What this has produced is a much smaller, leaner group of dedicated leaders who carry the fire with them. We still need those big "flame up" events and ideas. They provide some of the best moments in our journey together. But we must always return to the

(with each change adding a new gift just for me and a way to meet the requirements), I have known this is the place for me.

It's a privilege to work with the people I interact with daily, weekly, and monthly. The open heart of Christ is so very evident even as Evergreen does its ministry work. We leave meetings with a joy that comes through inviting and responding to the leading of Christ.

A former pastor of mine often ended church meetings by saying, "If all hearts are clear . . ." I now know the meaning of those words. It means that we are focused on the joy that is Christ and that we can all be at peace, in a safe place. Evergreen, including all who make up the Evergreen family of American Baptists, is just that kind of place, with that kind of atmosphere. It's home for me. Praised be the Lord!

core values that have inspired many to be so dedicated to the Association for so long.

Intentionally Inclusive at Work

When members of the task force formed by American Baptist Churches of the Northwest to establish a new region realized they did not represent the ethnic makeup of the churches that had been asked to form the new region, they determined to pull together a representative group. The group of churches (Seattle Baptist Union) asked to form a new region, approximately half were primarily African American in membership, approximately half were primarily Euro American, and a few were primarily Asian American. In contrast, the original task force had consisted of two male Asian American laity, one African American clergy (an associate pastor), and the rest were Euro American (one laywoman and three male clergy). I (a white clergywoman) was assigned to staff the group.

The task force decided to form a Vision Committee and asked each of the ethnic groups represented by the churches in Seattle

Voices of Evergreen

Lee Campbell is a member of Good Shepherd Baptist Church and a member of the Euro Caucus. She never served on the executive committee, but she came regularly to our annual meetings and for a while was her church's representative to the Association board. This was her witness in March 2013, on the occasion of Evergreen's tenth anniversary.

I have been involved with Evergreen since its inception, and I treasure the experiences and friendships that have become part of my life's journey. I have loving relationships with people I might

Baptist Union to send representatives to this Vision Committee. This committee was assigned three tasks: write a mission statement, come up with a name, and suggest a structure for the new region. Each ethnic group of churches (we didn't yet have caucuses) was asked to send up to four representatives. The Asian churches named two: one pastor and one male layperson. The African American churches named four clergy, all male, two of whom were always present at meetings; the other two came once or twice. The Euro-American churches sent two laywomen and one layman and (reluctantly on the part of the churches) one male associate pastor. The Vision Committee was much more representative of the churches than the task force.

I facilitated the Vision Committee, doing my best to remain in that role. I tried to be sure that everyone in the room had a voice in the process and that I did not intentionally influence the outcome. At the time, I knew very little about inclusive ministry or work. I did know something about group process but had done no reading about inclusive ministry specifically. However, I had a lot of relationships within the various groups represented at the table. And as someone

never have met if it weren't for the caucus structure of Evergreen. These friendships are ethnically and racially diverse. My life has been immeasurably enriched by the enduring, loving friendships created through the board, committees, appointments, and activities. In addition, I have learned so much from the governing technique of using consensus for the decision-making process.

Evergreen began out of some very painful and poor communications between people of faith. The birthing process was not only painful but arduous, requiring diligent effort on the part of many people. But as with many births, the results are magnificent.

I gratefully celebrate the current anniversary, and pray for many more to come.

trained in group processes, I knew our first task was getting to know one another and doing some basic work to build our relationships.

The first task was the mission statement. We worked on it for at least two full Saturdays. All of our meetings began with a Scripture reading and prayer led by one of the members. They usually shared why they selected the Scripture they did. The mission statement developed from the committee, and they edited it right up to the Constituting Convention where it was wholeheartedly adopted after adding the phrase, "and who value the liberties of our American Baptist heritage."

An Evergreen Story

Bob Fukano is a member of Japanese Baptist Church and the Asian Caucus. He was born behind barbed wire while his parents were interned during World War II. He served on the executive committee for four years and on the ministerial standards and concerns committee for six years. In May 2013 he gave this testi-

Voices of Evergreen

Any church in ABC-NW could choose to join what became Evergreen. Grace Baptist Church in Tacoma, Washington, was one of the congregations struggling with whether to join. Cathy Kernen was in seminary during that time. Several years later, after the previous pastor resigned and later passed away, Rev. Kernen became pastor, and Grace Baptist Church joined Evergreen. Her reflections appeared in September 2013 Evergreen Notes.

Belonging to the Evergreen Association has given our church an opportunity to partner with other churches that are diverse in ethnicity, practice, and polity. This diversity reminds us that the world is composed of Christ-followers who do not always look

mony, based on the Evergreen Association's Mission Statement (shown in italics below).

Mastering the Mission

> ***Evergreen Mission Preamble:*** *Being a culturally diverse people who are one in Christ and who value the liberties of our American Baptist heritage, the Evergreen Association of American Baptist Churches will:*
>
> ***Build bridges between communities.*** Evergreen introduced me to many people through a number of committees, gatherings, and programs. I like the people and it has been enjoyable and useful. I feel I can call them for advice and cooperation. I learned about their churches and some of their joys and struggles. They in turn learned a little about Japanese Baptist Church by meeting me. At our meetings, the caucuses pray together. Different communities lead prayer, and often it has been inspiring and a win-

like us physically, spiritually, and, dare I say, politically. We encounter conversations of the heart that open our world to a deeper and broader understanding of journeys that have not been our own, and we are invited to tell our own stories in a context of respect and caring. We welcome those who do not speak our language—either literally or figuratively—and we have grown in our understanding of the world as well as in our personal and corporate faith.

Belonging to the Evergreen Association has been a risky proposition as we make decisions with nontraditional approaches and extend ourselves and our churches to experience shared ministry in new ways. But from the challenges and the risks has been born a more beautiful picture of the Kingdom—here, now, and in heaven.

dow into the diverse ways of speaking to God. We have had fundraising events, barbeques, and other purely fun social activities. Nothing brings people closer together than having a good time! Evergreen's goal is to create a balanced relationship between racially diverse caucuses. I am inspired by that goal, knowing that the struggle for balance is real and continues.

Provide resources to equip member churches to share Christ and teach God's word. Evergreen has devoted its equipping efforts primarily to the formation of leadership. So far, it has seen mixed results to this challenging endeavor. The Evergreen staff has always been welcoming, and our executive minister always seeks the best resources for Evergreen leaders and churches to use. Leaders in the caucuses are drawn together for a variety of programs. I have served on the ministerial standards committee and participated in the process of recognizing the ordinations of several ministers. What I learned while on this committee is assisting me as I begin my role as moderator of Japanese Baptist Church.

Translate our unity to the world. The unity vision has not been completely realized, and it will always be a challenge given the liberty of each American Baptist congregation. However, the dedication of the caucuses, the faithfulness of the staff, and the understanding among churches are signs that the unity exists and has a place to grow.

An Evergreen Story

Rev. J. Manny Santiago, who is Puerto Rican, became a part of Evergreen when he was called as pastor of University Baptist Church, which is majority European. During his pastorate, Manny shared this testimony in June 2013.

When I first heard of Evergreen, I was in college. What I heard was pretty radical: Evergreen was an American Baptist region that intends to reflect and respect the Baptist principles of freedom, diversity, and mission. This sounded exciting! However, not in my wildest dreams did I think I would be a part of it. After all, I was four time zones, 3,900 miles, and two flight layovers away.

I grew up in the Iglesias Bautistas de Puerto Rico, and I was a delegate to the regional annual meeting when I first heard of Evergreen. The new region was expected to welcome churches that wanted to stay true to our Baptist principles and be a part of the larger American Baptist family. There was, however, a lot of misunderstanding—and shall I say, fears—about what exactly Evergreen meant and how it was going to work out. The project was something new and the ideas were quite radical: to be a nongeographical entity, made up of caucuses, working by consensus, with churches of very diverse theological positions. They would all have one thing in common: a commitment to mission.

Our denomination is diverse. We pride ourselves in saying that there is no clear ethnic majority among American Baptists. We have theologically liberal churches and theologically conservative churches, as well as everything in between. We consist of small churches and very large churches, multicultural churches, and churches that have kept their mission to a specific ethnic, cultural, or linguistic community. We have rural churches and urban churches, as well as churches that meet at homes and others that meet in cathedral-like buildings. Evergreen is home to churches from Alaska to California, from Utah to Venezuela. Evergreen is one of the regions in which you can find all this diversity!

To some extent, coming to Evergreen when I was called to be the pastor of University Baptist Church in Seattle was like coming home. Both the congregation and our region are places where I can share my ideas and thoughts openly and discuss issues that affect us all. I have been welcomed and affirmed by the region and by my colleagues at Evergreen. Our differences—of ethnicity, language, sexual orientation, and theological positions—are never downplayed but rather honored and affirmed. We might not see eye-to-eye on every single issue, but we are committed to take the time to listen and to understand one another better.

I am not saying that we face no challenges and that we are the perfect region. For instance, although Hispanic people have been part of Evergreen from the beginning, our current structure did not allow for a Hispanic caucus to be formed until recently. Yet we worked through it and listened to one another until we reached consensus and took positive actions. This, I believe, is an example of how the people who make up Evergreen let the spirit of Christ lead us in our work.

This is what Evergreen has meant to me: a place where the Spirit is allowed to lead us through the difficult conversations, the pleasant times of rejoicing, the painful growth processes, and the empowering communion of saints who are willing to walk this journey of life and faith together.

An Evergreen Story

Rev. Peter Koshi was the first Asian American pastor of Japanese Baptist Church's English-speaking congregation and served from 1956 to 1968. He stayed in the Seattle area as an educator and administrator retiring from Seattle Central

Voices of Evergreen

Lee Campbell is a member of Good Shepherd Baptist Church and a member of the Euro Caucus. She never served on the executive committee, but she came regularly to our annual meetings and for a while was her church's representative to the Association board. This was her witness in March 2013, on the occasion of Evergreen's tenth anniversary.

I have been involved with Evergreen since its inception, and I treasure the experiences and friendships that have become part of my life's journey. I have loving relationships with people I might never have met if it weren't for the caucus structure of Evergreen. These friendships are ethnically and racially diverse. My life has been immeasurably enriched by the enduring, loving friendships created through the board, committees, appointments, and activities. In addition, I have learned so much from the governing technique of using consensus for the decision-making process.

Evergreen began out of some very painful and poor communications between people of faith. The birthing process was not only painful but arduous, requiring diligent effort on the part of many people. But as with many births, the results are magnificent.

I gratefully celebrate the current anniversary, and pray for many more to come.

Community College. He passed away in 2016, buried with an Evergreen stole around his neck. Yosh Nakagawa was excited when Rev. Koshi agreed to serve as Evergreen's first Asian chair for the 2006–2007 term. He wrote articles for our monthly newsletter, and what follows is one of his best.

In this time just before Easter 2007, it seems fitting that I lift up the strength of Evergreen Association of ABCUSA. Being bridges as members of Evergreen, and building bridges is truly a remarkable undertaking and focus of our Association.

One might ask, "Why spend time building bridges when we're doing well?" A poem by Will Allen Dromgoole, "The Bridge Builder," verses two and three, comes to mind:

> "Old man," said a fellow pilgrim near,
> "You are wasting your strength building here;
> Your journey will end with the ending day,
> You never again will pass this way,
> You've crossed the chasm deep and wide,
> Why build you this bridge at evening tide?"
>
> The builder lifted his old gray head,
> "Good friend, in the path I have come," he said,
> "There followeth after me today
> A youth whose feet must pass this way.
> This chasm which has been as naught to me
> To that fair-haired youth might a pitfall be,
> He, too, must cross in the twilight dim,
> Good friend, I am building the bridge for him."

Don't we wish that someone had built a bridge for us Baptists so that we would not fail to cross the "chasm" deep and wide as many are doing?

What an ingenious concept for a region to lift up! Who thought of such an idea? Or is it more accurate to attribute it to inspiration of the Holy Spirit? A bridge not only connects but overrides torrents, barriers, or obstructions, making access possible from opposite sides—the bridge becoming the common ground.

May I suggest some "bridging words": *respect for, identifying with, relating with,* and *shalom.* The two most powerful bridge words are—*peace*, the proclamation of the Angels, ". . . and peace on earth to all whom God favors" (Luke 2:14, NLT), and *love,* as Jesus said, "This is my commandment, that you love one another as I have loved you" (John 15:12, NRSV).

Jesus, the Christ, is our bridge to the Father and the Father's bridge to us. Hallelujah, Christ is risen, indeed! Happy Easter to all!

An Evergreen Story

Rev. Dr. Patricia Hunter has long served American Baptists as a representative of the Ministers and Missionaries Benefit Board. She is a member of the Black Caucus and an associate minister of her lifelong home church, Mount Zion Baptist Church, Seattle. Her testimony appeared in May 2014.

I am grateful that a Baptist region like Evergreen exists. Evergreen understands that ministry in urban settings must be diverse for the gospel to be heard in various communities. Each Evergreen church is unique in its quest to spread the love of God. Evergreen churches come in various sizes, speak many languages, and sing every style of sacred music from gospel rap to anthems of praise.

Evergreen churches are racially and theologically diverse, and the region's leadership reflects that diversity. Seldom do ministry organizations work diligently to have all constituents at the table ***and*** have their voices heard. Often, a few officers are willing to direct the many without real input or consideration of varying voices. Evergreen is different.

Voices of Evergreen

Bob Sittig has served as both treasurer and chair of Evergreen from the Euro Caucus. He is a member and retired administrator of Seattle First Baptist Church. His final reflection as chair follows.

When folks leave various positions in organizations, they often use the word *bittersweet* to describe their feelings about departing. Because there is no bitter for me, I can only use the word *sweet* to characterize my feelings as I step down from my post. Our diversity and the common bonds we share make Evergreen an example for all regions. Practices that separate people from one another because of insular beliefs are not what God has in mind for us, and they can only cause strife among us. Evergreen demonstrates a different way, which I believe will result in our continued growth.

We have accomplished a great deal during my two-year tenure. Recognizing and supporting a sister church in Venezuela and continuing to grow our organization by the addition of several churches during this period are just two of the accomplishments that have sweetened this work. From the work of Rev. Dr. Marcia Patton, ministering to all the pastors in the Evergreen family in ways seen and unseen, to the work of Clem Winbush, taking care of the myriad of administrative duties with a cheerful attitude—all these actions, both big and small, add up to a significant demonstration of Evergreen doing God's work in a world in such desperate need.

The process of Evergreen's birth was painful. The split over whether to allow Welcoming and Affirming churches in the Region was unfortunate. I am sure God was not pleased with the behavior of many. The verbal venom spewed by those who claimed to know Jesus was soul damaging. At times I was not sure whether love would win, but ten years later Evergreen is a witness that God is faithful.

There is a gospel song entitled, "At the Table." The song says that at the feast of the Lord, we find peace and joy and love around the table. I am grateful that God welcomes me daily to that great feast. Yes, there is room for all at God's table and at Evergreen's table as well. Hallelujah!

An Evergreen Story

Curtis Price was one of the Euro Caucus members of the Vision Committee, and the first chair of Evergreen named by the Euro Caucus. He wrote the piece that follows in October 2008, after six years with Evergreen and during the last months of his service as chair. He demonstrates the spirit that it is "all about relationships." We end this chapter and the exploration of inclusive ministry with his reflections.

> What can be done to make sure all voices are brought to the table? Our ministry together is built on a foundation of relationship. At its deepest level our connection one to another is as brothers and sisters in Christ. In Evergreen we take this relationship to heart and have found many creative ways to nurture deep relationships.
>
> We are exploring new ways of being. Our structure has brought with it many interesting opportunities. I have made relationships and worked with colleagues with whom in the past I would rarely have met, let alone become friends. In addition to putting me in contact with people of different racial and ethnic cultures than my own, our structure has also given me the opportunity to consider my own racial and ethnic culture. We in the Euro Caucus are in the unfamiliar territory of asking, "What

does it mean for us to be a group?" and "How can we include all of the voices in our own cultural community?" I take comfort in the fact that people in the other caucuses have similar struggles. The struggle is a good one.

Being Evergreen has meant that controversial issues are never allowed to highjack the process or sidetrack the ministry. It is not that we are without controversy. In fact, the same conversations happen here that are happening everywhere. However, instead of setting up two microphones and letting people line up behind them to show the veracity of their position, we work to create an environment of listening to each other and sharing our own heart in an effort to seek the mind of Christ. Through tools such as the RESPECT Communication Guidelines and working in small table groups, we come closer to creating an equitable exchange of ideas.

American Baptists take great pride in the claim that we are the most racially and ethnically diverse denomination. Finally, in Evergreen, we are embracing this boast and making it a real priority.

Questions for Reflection

1. What can you do in your own life to cultivate meaningful relationships with people who are racially, culturally, theologically, or otherwise different from you?
2. What can you do to create such relationships in your local church or community?

EXCURSUS

How Did It All Begin?

Evergreen Association created a new way of doing things that has brought a sense of inclusion to many who had not experienced it before. Our work in caucuses by consensus has created something beyond what any of us thought it would when we decided to go that direction. That's the real story. But behind those decisions is a another story of why the group of churches in Seattle Baptist Union (SBU) was even asked to form a new region in the first place.

We must go back to the formation of American Baptist Churches of the Northwest (ABC-NW) to understand in part how Evergreen came into being. In the late 1970s American Baptist Churches went through a reorganization of the structure of the denomination after a study of regional relationships. The recommendation of the study was that the Northwest should be made up of Oregon Baptist Convention, Washington Baptist Convention (WBC), and Idaho Baptist Convention. However, Oregon decided that it did not want to join with Washington Baptist Convention but would instead stand on its own. The study also recommended that the North Dakota Baptist Convention and South Dakota Baptist Convention should join with the Montana Baptist Convention. However, both the Dakotas decided initially that they wanted to stand on their own and had no interest in joining with Montana. Meanwhile, the plan recommended that the Colorado and Wyoming Conventions join with Utah Baptist Association, but what would be the new Rocky Mountain Region had no interest in including Utah. So the Washington-Idaho Convention welcomed Montana and Utah. In the seventies and eighties, they also included the Alaska churches, making the Northwest Region the largest geographically in the United States, including even the new American Baptist Churches of the South.

In many of the reorganized Regions of American Baptist Churches, the old conventions were simply reorganized into the new Regions. In ABC-NW none of the old conventions went away. They became the property holders and ABC-NW became the programming arm of the churches in the area. For example, Utah Baptist Association, which was the legal owner of UTABA, a campground outside of Ogden, continued to hold that property and others. The agreement among the executives of each of the conventions was that the executive of Washington Baptist Convention would be the first executive of the new ABC-NW region. And because of convenience, because Washington Baptist Convention owned the office, the region office would be located in Seattle in the Washington Baptist Convention office building.

At the time of this agreement, WBC had approximately a hundred and fifty churches, more than one hundred of them west of the Cascades; Montana Baptist Convention had about forty churches; and Idaho Baptist Convention about the same. Utah Baptist Association had about ten. In the years preceding this "reorganization," Idaho, Montana, and Utah had worked together before as a group, so this was not unprecedented, but it *was* unprecedented that the main offices were so far from many local churches.

In addition to the four state conventions, another entity had long been in existence but had no part of the organizational structure of Washington Baptist Convention or ABC-NW. It consisted of approximately forty American Baptist churches in a specific geography in and around Seattle and was called Seattle Baptist Union (SBU). Over time, SBU had accumulated a small legacy of funds from which it made small grants to local churches to help them get new initiatives started. In the years before the formation of

Evergreen, SBU had given some assistance to the work and ministry of ABC-NW. The Region never seriously considered relocating the offices from Seattle, but there was tension under the surface in Idaho, Montana, and Utah that the Region office was so far away, as well as a belief that Washington churches, and Seattle churches in particular, controlled everything. There was even a sense that one church in particular, Seattle First Baptist, held sway over all others. (You will not find that in records but the sentiment was voiced in gatherings over the years.)

In the 1990s American Baptist Churches USA General Board was under pressure to adopt a statement about homosexuality. Consequently, the following statement was adopted by the General Board of ABCUSA by mail vote (the only mail vote ever taken on a policy statement) in October 1992 with 110 in favor, 64 opposed, and 5 abstaining: "We affirm that the practice of homosexuality is incompatible with Christian teaching."

It was in this context that University Baptist Church of Seattle, Washington, a member of American Baptist Churches (and therefore part of ABC-NW, WBC, and SBU), called a pastor who was, in addition to being called, qualified, and spiritually gifted, openly gay. University Baptist Church was a member of the fairly new Association of Welcoming and Affirming Baptists (AWAB), one of the two churches in ABC-NW to be a part of that body. The other church was also in Seattle, First Baptist Church.

In the late 1990s there had been a growing underground concern about these two churches from outside the Seattle area. In 1996 American Baptist Churches of the West had dis-fellowshipped four churches from their Region because they were members of AWAB. Perhaps ABC-NW could have continued with some concerns about the two churches being members of AWAB, but the calling of a pastor who was openly gay ignited a flame. It should be noted that this pastor was not an ordained American Baptist. American Baptist Churches are free to call whomever they choose and are limited only by the local church bylaws, not by any agreement with American Baptist Churches. The pastor called by University Baptist Church had been ordained in the church in which he grew up, a Baptist General Conference Church in Michigan. He had not yet gone through a process of having that ordination recognized by American Baptist Churches. However, those details did not matter to those in ABC-NW who were concerned about his presence among the clergy in the region.

Let me reiterate that local American Baptist churches may call whomsoever they choose. There are no regulations from American Baptist Churches USA that require that local congregations call only American Baptist-ordained or recognized pastors. The reason for this is the Baptist tenet of local church autonomy. The local church has the right to form its own bylaws and is not bound by any decisions made by other American Baptists, locally or nationally, except those which it freely chooses to adopt, such as its decision to be associated with American Baptists.

This particular controversy put the tenet of local church autonomy in tension with another Baptist distinctive: that of soul liberty, by which each individual believer is responsible for interpreting Scripture according to one's own understanding of the Spirit and text. Therefore, those who interpreted Scripture to understand homosexuality (in and of itself) as an abomination, viewed those who identified as lesbian, gay, bisexual, or transgender as unrepentant sinners who should not and could not serve as pastors or leaders in the church in any form. However, there were no specific documents within ABC-NW or ABCUSA that specifically prohibited a church from being a member of AWAB or from calling a pastor who identified as gay.

The executive minister of ABC-NW sent a letter to all churches in the Region in December 1996 informing them that University Baptist Church had called a part-time pastor who was openly gay. In response, the ABC-NW Region Board passed the following at their meeting in April 1997:

> ABC-NW affirms the authority of Scripture in the lives of our churches and members, though we acknowledge that there are various interpretations and applications of Scripture among us.
>
> We affirm that Jesus Christ died to take away the sin of the whole world.
>
> We affirm the need for the various and sometimes differing voices among our churches and people which, as we hear them, can help to balance, correct, and complete our spiritual understandings. We affirm the right of the local church to listen to its individual members' understandings of Scripture that contribute to its life and ministry.
>
> We recognize that there are serious issues, which could divide us, but the issues raised do not compel us to take action which could lead to the dismissal of a congregation.
>
> In the spirit of this statement, we acknowledge that there are many behaviors, including the practice of homosexuality, which are inconsistent with Christian teaching. We do not, however, believe that the breaking of relationship with Churches is consistent with the will of God.

Then in their November Board meeting (the ABC-NW Board met twice a year), the Board released the following statement: "While we acknowledge that the ordination and calling of a pastor are functions of the local church, ABC Northwest will not grant recognition of ordination of a practicing gay or lesbian person." And then in March, two months before the Biennial Convention in Spokane, they adopted the "We Are American Baptists" as their statement of faith. (The full text of this statement can be found in Appendix B.)

The leaders of churches, particularly in Southern Idaho, but indeed all around ABC-NW, began to call for action against the AWAB churches in the Region. The 1998 Biennial Convention of

ABC-NW was held in Spokane, for the first time at a hotel instead of a local congregation because no church in the Spokane area was equipped to handle the large convention. As the convention approached, several amendments were brought that would have set up a way to dismiss the two churches. Rev. Dr. Bob Roberts was the speaker for the convention. Although none of his efforts at mediation were in and of themselves controversial, the convention had a mood of confrontation. To add to the sense of unease, someone had informed the Spokane media that the Baptists were arguing and they thought that required media presence. Although media were not allowed in the meeting room, the encounters outside the meeting room were tense. A parliamentarian was present for all of the debated meeting.

As a staff member, I did not spend a lot of time in the business meeting, but while there I observed that during the debates, not only did one side not listen to the other, but the sides did not listen to those who spoke before or after them on their own side of the issue. In the end, all the proposals were removed from the agenda. However, an informational directive was passed during a meeting that went beyond the stated meeting time. It resulted in a directive from the ABC-NW board that met the following October:

> #1 We call on all individuals and churches to proclaim God's grace and forgiveness and to speak out against violence of all kinds, including against persons of all sexual orientations. We encourage churches to consult with Region staff and Area Board to obtain curriculum and programs that address these issues.
>
> #2 ABC-NW reaffirms the following: There are many behaviors, including the practice of homosexuality, which are inconsistent with Christian teaching. The ordination and calling of a pastor are functions of the local church.

> The Region will not grant recognition of ordination to a practicing gay or lesbian person.
>
> #3 The Region Board, through this communication, continues to call all churches into conformity with Region Policies.
>
> #4 The Region Board and staff will not support any program that describes homosexual practice as an acceptable Christian lifestyle.

This created a reluctant truce by the time we had a service that included Communion at the end of the meeting. Everyone went home grateful that the Region was intact but feeling that its stability was tenuous at best, and that if everyone did not cooperate by refusing to fan the embers, the Region would not last. Clearly no one had gotten what they wanted: those who wanted the AWAB churches out still had them in the Region, and the two AWAB churches did not feel like they could carry out their ministry without concern that the Region would take exception to what they were doing.

The churches of Utah and Southern Idaho were in the Intermountain Area, one of the five areas of the ABC-NW. During its fall 1999 meeting, the Intermountain Area passed a statement making it clear that if a church was an AWAB church, it would dismiss itself from the fellowship. They carefully followed the guidelines that set up this statement as an amendment to the ABC-NW bylaws.

This action by the Intermountain Area was a disappointment to the ABC-NW staff, as we had been hoping to avoid another meeting like the one in Spokane in 1998. With this amendment coming, we tried to circumvent a repeat of the Spokane convention with the upcoming Regional meeting held at First Baptist Church, Salt Lake City, Utah.

We invited thirty people to a forty-eight-hour event at Ross Point Camp in Post Falls, Idaho, one of the camps WBC owned. We collectively made a list of ten people from each of the "opposing" sides (which included the pastors of the two churches that were members of AWAB and authors of the proposed bylaw change from Southern Idaho) and then invited ten people from the "middle." We contracted with Mennonite Central Committee to send a couple of people to facilitate the meeting.

The staff's hope for this meeting was that we could listen to one another well enough to take the proposed changes to the bylaws off the table. However, we came to an impasse when those representatives who had proposed the bylaw change refused to withdraw it unless the two churches agreed to leave AWAB. (Even so, the representatives would have to go back to the congregations that had asked for the bylaw change and could not guarantee that outcome even if the churches did leave AWAB.) But that proved to be moot, because the representatives of the two AWAB churches similarly indicated they could not speak for their congregations; they would have to go back to their membership for a decision, and the representatives did not think it likely that they would vote to leave AWAB, particularly under the pressure to keep peace.

The Mennonite team that was facilitating the meeting worked further with the group, and an agreement was forged that put the following resolution before the May 2000 Convention: "With deep regret, we acknowledge that a reorganization of the Region is necessary, and call for a regional process, including the proposed self-study, to determine the configuration of the new regional structure, to be determined on or before May 2002."

At the May 2000 meeting in Salt Lake City, the proposed bylaw change from the Intermountain Area Churches failed (by a handful of votes) to reach the necessary two-thirds majority required by the existing bylaws. But the resolution passed by 80 percent of the voting delegates.

That resulted in a meeting at Ross Point Camp in November 2000 of seventy-four representatives. Although more people of color were invited by the staff, only two Asian American laity, one Asian American clergy, and one African American layperson attended. The other seventy were all Caucasian. The current chair of SBU was present, and he suggested that perhaps SBU churches could form a new region, and that idea was affirmed. Later the ABC-NW Board also affirmed the decision and two task forces were formed, one for the continuing region and one for the new region.

Reflecting on the Conflict

The conflict was (as most conflicts are) multidimensional. Different issues affected the actions of those who engaged the conflict. Some churches felt that their own biblical understanding of sexuality and gender identity was important. Other congregations, even though they may have disagreed with the biblical understanding of the AWAB churches, supported the Baptist tenet of local church autonomy; therefore, they were unwilling to support a regional bylaw change that would have ousted the churches that were only doing ministry in their context as they believed they were called by God to do.

The new region task force realized that the leadership (pastors) in SBU did not know one another. Some large churches in the area were going through shifts in leadership resulting from the retirement of several long-serving African American pastors, and new pastors were beginning to take their places. The Euro American churches in SBU were experiencing a similar shift; although the pastorates weren't as long, some of the longest-serving pastors were retiring, and others had left. The Asian churches were also experiencing change in pastoral leadership. One African American pastor remarked to me during that time, "We don't know each other, so why would we trust you?"

So, instead of immediately putting together bylaws, the task force decided to build some events so that "we might get to know each other." The task force sponsored a dinner cruise as well as an outing to a baseball game. These efforts, among others over the year, helped the people who lived near one another to get to know each other. At the end of that year the task force asked the Vision Committee to do its work.

While all this was going on in ABC-NW, American Baptist Church USA was dealing with the fallout of the four churches that had been "disfellowshipped" from American Baptist Churches of the West. These were churches in good standing with American Baptist Churches; they participated in programs, they gave to American Baptist mission concerns, their pastors were ordained in American Baptist Churches, and they were in the retirement benefit program of American Baptist Churches (the Ministers and Missionaries Benefit Board). An agreement was reached after much debate to allow these churches to remain in American Baptist Churches if they could find other region homes. They did. One church found a home with the American Baptist Churches of Metro New York, another with Philadelphia Baptist Association, the third with American Baptist Churches of Rochester Genesee, and the fourth with the American Baptist Churches of Wisconsin.

A number of other churches in the greater San Francisco area joined these four and formed the Pacific Coast Baptist Association. Initially this group was working toward becoming a region. Several other churches regularly met with them. At the very beginning of this work, the two churches in Seattle that were members of AWAB were included because they were none too certain whether or not they, too, might be dismissed from the current American Baptist region of which they were a part. Even though the four churches found new regional church homes, Pacific Coast Baptist Association continued to work toward becoming a region.

ABCUSA's reaction to this movement was to develop a process by which a new region of churches could be accepted into the American Baptist family. These new procedures were adopted by the General Executive Council (all executive ministers of regions of American Baptist Churches, the general secretary, the treasurer, and at least one other staff member from the general secretary's office, and the executive directors of International Ministries, the American Baptist Home Mission Societies, the Ministers and Missionaries Benefit Board, American Baptist Women's Ministries and the American Baptist Historical Society, the Ministers Council, and a few others) and recommended to the General Board, which adopted them. About the same time ABC-NW had assigned a task force to create a new region with Seattle Baptist Union churches, newly adopted this procedure was put in place.

The procedure called for a two-step process. The first step was to submit paperwork and be accepted by the General Executive Council as a provisional region. The second step, which could not be taken until at least a year later but not more than two, would be to again go before the General Executive Council, which would recommend (or not) that the body be accepted as a region with American Baptist Churches USA.

The General Executive Council had been working for several years to put forward a new Budget Covenant between the various ABC entities. It was Rev. Dr. Roy Medley's first General Executive Council as general secretary. At the end of this long week came the proposal from the task force asking the GEC to give the new region in the Seattle area (not yet named at the time) provisional status. The procedures required at least a two-thirds majority vote for the measure to pass. When the voting took place, the only reason a two-thirds majority was achieved was because Roy Medley cast a vote. As the convener of the GEC, he usually would not vote. In this case he did, and the fledgling organization had the go-ahead to become a provisional region.

Six to seven weeks later, the Constituting Convention was held in Tacoma in May 2002 and the name Evergreen Association was selected. According to the process for becoming a region, the next

April a petition was made to the GEC to recommend to the ABCUSA General Board that Evergreen Association be a region of ABCUSA.

The General Executive Council met in April 2003 outside of Prague, Czech Republic. This time the agenda was shorter and lighter than it had been a year before. The proposal was passed with everyone voting to affirm, with two abstentions. That sent the proposal to the General Board, which was meeting in Richmond, Virginia, before the Biennial Convention of ABCUSA scheduled there.

Yosh, as vice-president, was seated with the other ABCUSA officers on a dais in the room where the 120 voting delegates were meeting. I made a presentation that reviewed our mission statement and structure. During the question-and-answer period after the presentation, one of the representatives from ABC-NW actually spoke against the motion. A couple of questions later, Patti Stratton, one of the representatives from American Baptist Churches of Maine, asked if the churches of Evergreen believed in Jesus Christ as Lord and Savior, and I replied simply, "Certainly." Very soon after this the vote was called. The vote was 74 yes, 27 no, and 19 abstentions.

With that number of abstentions, the president did not immediately call the vote but consulted with the parliamentarian. Before the delegates convened for the day (to gather again after other meetings a-day-and-half later), it was announced that the vote was secured for Evergreen to be recognized as a region of the American Baptist Churches USA. The president and general secretary were authorized to countersign the Covenant of Relationships with Evergreen Association on behalf of the ABCUSA. There was an Evergreen delegation at the Biennial that followed these meetings, and we were rejoicing throughout!

Many in the wider ABC family assumed that all churches making up the new region were Welcoming and Affirming. To my knowledge, though, no one ever asked. If asked, the answer was that only two AWAB churches were part of the new region. It wasn't even that all the churches were in agreement about the "homosexual issue." Some churches in Seattle Baptist Union became Evergreen because they didn't want to make a decision, so they just went along with automatically becoming a part of the new region. Others liked the idea of doing region work with nearby churches rather than the larger ABC-NW geography. Many chose not to be aware of the changes that were coming one way or another.

An exchange I had with one African American pastor while these discussions were going on went like this:

> *Me:* "The new region is not designed to be a Welcoming and Affirming Region. It will have two churches that are members of AWAB, but they just want to do their ministry as they see fit."
>
> *Pastor:* "They don't want to come into my church and tell me how to do ministry there?"
>
> *Me:* "That's correct. They just want to do their ministry and not be threatened by expulsion if they do."
>
> *Pastor:* "That sounds Baptist to me. As long as they don't want to tell me how to do my ministry, I don't have any desire to tell them how to do theirs."

Final Thoughts

When ABC-NW made the decision to ask SBU to form a new region, I thought for sure that we had made a big mistake; I was convinced that the task force had been given a peck of lemons. But I learned that God can make wonderful things from lemons: lemonade, lemon drops, lemon pie!

ABC-NW gave Evergreen the gift of a blank slate. The decision of the group of 72 at Ross Point and the ABC-NW board did not give any particular guidelines for formation of the new region.

That blank slate gave the new region task force and what became Evergreen the option to try new things. It was a wonderful gift.

By taking time in 2002 to get to know one another rather than immediately racing to the details of bylaws, we gave ourselves the additional gift of perspective to see that the original task force was not the best representative group to make next recommendations. No one was telling us we needed adaptive change. It was the work of God that created the collective wisdom to take time before we began the work. It was the work of God that brought together the Vision Committee. It was the work of God in the Vision Committee that inspired the mission statement, name, and caucus structure. It was the work of God that gave us courage to adopt consensus as our process for decision-making.

Evergreen has valued our learning in the years since the experiment began. The learning continues. Our prayer is that this book will bring hope to many and offer insight and suggestions to those who are seeking to do inclusive ministry.

Epilogue

> That we may be mutually encouraged by each other's faith, both yours and mine. (Romans 1:12)

In 2016, in preparation for my transition to retirement, the Evergreen Association conducted a study among our pastors and church members. We found overwhelming support for continuing our caucus structure and for working by consensus. Indeed, both were considered nonnegotiable. The fact that we have made significant strides in moving people from tolerating others to deeply appreciating people different from themselves stands out to the pastors and people of Evergreen as being our most significant accomplishment.

Part of our mission statement holds that we will "translate our unity to the world." This rather audacious mission statement has been reflected in our work, and the people of Evergreen believe we have done just that. They use words and phrases such "inclusion," "you are welcome," "unity in our diversity," and "harmony not unison" to describe the ways in which our vision has come alive in the world. The unity that we sought has been largely achieved: people feel welcomed, experience harmony, and expect diversity.

In our work in Evergreen, generally our answer to "Can we?" is "Yes!" As long as there is a "we" and the work suggested brings God's love to the world, we try to be a positive people. Our attempts at developing an inclusive ministry number more than these pages. We are delighted that we have come this far, and we sing with others that "we have come this far by faith, leaning on the Lord." To be sure, we haven't done it alone.

We have experienced significant growth. The Association has expanded from an original twenty-seven churches in and around Seattle, plus one each in eastern Washington and Northern Idaho, to a total of fifty-five churches. Ten of them are in California, two in Utah, one in Alaska, one in Northern Idaho, and one in Colorado, and the remaining forty are in Washington. We are even in relationship with a church in Venezuela![1]

Evergreen sponsors events each year in the Seattle area. On Martin Luther King Jr. Day each year we host a worship event in the evening with insightful preachers who bring a challenge to serve and be a voice for the marginalized. Recently we have gathered an inclusive choir across Seattle area churches, and each year their voices grow! Annually the Black Caucus hosts a barbeque with food and fellowship that would rival anything you have experienced. We also gather with the Hispanic Caucus around Cinco de Mayo to celebrate and sing a little in Spanish. Just for fun we attend a Mariner's baseball game together as a region. (Yosh helped us get that started fifteen years ago.) We rejoice when our members from our growing number of churches of people from Burma attend. We only wish there were a way to include our geographically scattered churches in these events.

In addition to numerical growth, we have grown in the grace and wisdom of God. We began with having no idea that our work would be a story worth telling. Relying on God and one another, we took each step trusting that we would learn. There were some missteps and much learning—and many occasions when the learning happened without missteps!

Evergreen was blessed at the beginning with a blank slate: no existing bylaws, no existing structure that we had to adapt. Instead we could dream and create an association that was inclusive of all American Baptist people who desired to "do church" while being faithful to God's call to diversity and inclusion. We have worked to be sure that all voices are heard, and that everyone is not only at the table but has a hand in putting the table together. We still have to work at it.

Evergreen continues to learn how to be inclusive. But whatever has been and will be accomplished is by God's grace and wisdom guiding us. We pray that in telling our story, you have found some guidance for achieving inclusion in your organization, and that you may add to the narrative of building a table for intentionally inclusive ministry.

APPENDIX A

Bylaws of the Evergreen Association of American Baptist Churches

ARTICLE I.
MISSION
Being a culturally diverse people who are one in Christ and who value the liberties of our American Baptist heritage, the Evergreen Association of American Baptist Churches will build bridges between communities; provide resources to equip member churches to share Christ and teach God's word; and translate our unity to the world.

ARTICLE II.
MEMBERS
1. Qualifications for Membership. The Membership shall be comprised of American Baptist Churches that meet the American Baptist Churches, USA ("ABC/USA") Common Criteria:

(1) Affirm the statement entitled, "We Are American Baptists," revised June 19, 1998, as it may be amended;
(2) Affirm the mission and purpose of the American Baptist Churches USA and of Evergreen Baptist Association;
(3) Participate in the life and mission of the American Baptist Churches at local, regional, national, and international levels;

(4) Financially support the mission of the American Baptist Churches at a responsible level; and

(5) Share with the family the impact of the church's mission in reaching the community and world for Christ by reporting annually on forms supplied by the region and/or American Baptist Churches USA.

2. Delegate Rights. Each member church shall be entitled to five official delegates per church provided that the church meets the membership guidelines outlined in section 1 above including contribution to American Baptist Mission and submission of the annual report form. Each church may also send an unlimited number of members to meetings who are not official delegates.

Each Delegate and that Delegate's mailing address shall be affirmed to represent the church upon the signature of such church's pastor or clerk.

ARTICLE III.

MEETINGS OF THE MEMBERSHIP

1. Annual Meeting. A Convention of the Members shall be held annually in the month of October. The purpose of the Annual Meeting shall be to elect the Officers (as nominated by the Caucuses), nominate ABC/USA Mission Table and Board of General Ministries Nominees, approve the Association's annual budget, approve membership and welcome new Caucuses, approve membership and welcome new churches, review of the actions of the Association Board and Executive Committee, and for the transaction of other business as may properly come before the Annual Meeting.

2. Special Meetings. Special meetings of the Members, as deemed necessary for the competent management of the Association, may be called at the request of a caucus or at the request of the Chair and two-thirds (2/3) of the members of the Executive Committee. A special meeting shall be held for the calling of an Executive Minister.

3. Notice. Notices of Annual and special meetings shall be mailed to each Member Church at least one (1) month prior to any meeting. The business to be transacted, or the purpose of, any meeting of the Members needs to be specified in the notice of such meeting.

4. Quorum. A majority of the number of Delegates registered for a meeting provided at least one delegate from each caucus is present shall constitute a quorum for the transaction of business at any Member meeting. In the absence of the Chair and Vice Chair, the quorum present may choose a chairperson for the meeting. In the absence of a quorum, the Delegates present will adjourn the meeting. Participation by a Delegate in a meeting by a conference telephone or other electronic communications equipment by means of which all persons participating may hear each other at the same time shall constitute presence at the meeting of such Delegates.

5. Manner of Acting. The decisions and acts of the membership shall be made by consensus unless noted otherwise. Consensus is a deliberative process where collective decisions are arrived at by a group of individuals working together for the good of the organization and its mission. Conditions under which consensus is formed include open communication in a supportive climate that gives the participants a sense that they have had a fair chance to influence the decision and that all group members understand and support the decision. Consensus building means that all participants listen carefully and communicate effectively. Consensus has been reached when all parties can at least live with the decision and will agree to support the decision of the body.

ARTICLE IV.
CAUCUSES

The framers of the Evergreen Baptist Association are desirous of the day when racial/ethnic equality is a reality, at least within the Association circle. Until that day, it is deemed that special action is needed to ensure voice and representation across racial/ethnic lines, therefore:

1. Caucus Membership. [The 2003 Adopted Bylaws had this sentence as the first in this article: *Each Member church must choose to become a member of a particular Caucus subject to the approval of the caucus.* It was removed in a bylaw change adopted at the 2013 Annual Meeting.] Caucuses are formed in relationship to national American Baptist caucuses (except Euro-American) and which have a population within the Association. Caucuses with representation at this time are African American, Asian American, Hispanic and Euro American caucuses. Once a caucus forms, organizes, and meets, it may ask to be a regular caucus and request welcome and recognition with all the rights and responsibilities outlined below.

2. Caucus Responsibilities. The Caucuses shall teach all members regarding the American Baptist Family and cooperate with the ABC National Caucus groups. They shall also establish agendas for the Association Board and the Membership Annual Meetings including programs, outreach, and visioning, and recommend new churches and church plants to the Association Board. In addition, each Caucus shall select two (2) representatives from Association Churches to serve on the Executive Committee and from whom officers shall be chosen on a rotating basis.

ARTICLE V.
ASSOCIATION BOARD

1. General Powers. The Association Board shall be responsible for the general program of the Association including but not limited to: vision of the Association, proposing budget, supervision of the Executive Minister, review the actions of the Executive Committee which the Association Board deems appropriate, and recommending new churches. The Association Board will name a search committee for Executive Minister.

2. Number and Qualification. The Board of the Association shall be composed of:

(i) One (1) representative from each member church;

(ii) The Executive Committee;

(iii) One (1) representative from each national ABC caucus that has a constituency within the Association which has not yet formed a Caucus within the Association (i.e., the Native American national caucuses), until such time as such group forms a Caucus recognized by the Association, after which it will have all the rights and responsibilities of the other Caucuses; and

(iv) The ABC/USA Board of General Ministries Representative.

3. Committees. Standing or temporary committees may be appointed by the Board from time to time from its own number or from church members of member churches. The Board may from time to time invest such committees with such powers as it may see fit, subject to such conditions as may be prescribed by such Board. All committees so appointed shall keep regular minutes of the transactions of their meetings and shall cause them to be recorded in books kept for that purpose in the office of the Association. The designation of any such committee and the delegation of authority thereto shall not relieve the Board, or any member thereof, of any responsibilities imposed by law.

a. The Ministerial Standards and Concerns Committee shall be a regular standing committee that will supervise recognition of ordination and give oversight to accusations of ethical violations of recognized ordained persons.

4. Regular Meetings. The Association Board shall hold meetings at least quarterly on a date to be scheduled at the discretion of the Chair and may be within or outside the State of Washington.

5. Special Meetings. Special meetings of the Association Board, as deemed necessary for the competent management of the Association,

may be called at the request of a caucus or at the request of the Chair and two-thirds (2/3) of the Executive Committee.

6. Notice. Notices of regular meetings shall be mailed or emailed to all Board Members at least two (2) weeks prior to any meeting. Notice of any special Board meeting shall be mailed or emailed at least one (1) week prior to any such special meeting. It shall be deemed to be delivered when deposited in the United States mail, properly addressed with postage prepaid or sent to their regularly used email address.

7. Quorum. A majority of the number of Board Members fixed by Article V, paragraph 2, shall constitute a quorum for the transaction of business at any Board meeting provided there are present at least one representative from each sitting caucus. In the absence of the Chair and Vice Chair, the quorum present may choose a chairperson for the meeting. In the absence of a quorum, a majority of the Board Members present will adjourn the meeting. Participation by a member in a meeting by a conference telephone or other electronic communications equipment by means of which all persons participating may hear each other at the same time shall constitute presence at the meeting of such a Board Member.

8. Manner of Acting. The decisions and acts of the Board Members shall be made by consensus unless noted otherwise.

ARTICLE VI.
EXECUTIVE COMMITTEE

1. General Powers. The business, property and affairs of the Association shall be vested in the member churches and is managed by the Executive Committee. In addition to the powers granted by the Articles of Incorporation and by these Bylaws, the Executive Committee may exercise all such powers and perform all such lawful acts as are not prohibited by statute or by the Articles of Incorporation or by these Bylaws.

2. Members of the Executive Committee. The Executive Committee shall be composed of the following members:

(i) The two (2) representatives from each Caucus from whom the officers are nominated and

(ii) The Executive Minister.

The Executive Committee shall have and exercise all of the authority of the Association Board and shall make decisions when the entire Association Board does not meet. The Executive Committee shall keep regular minutes of the transactions of their meetings and shall cause them to be recorded in books kept for that purpose in the office of the Association. The designation of any such committee and the delegation of authority thereto shall not relieve the Board, or any member thereof, of any responsibilities imposed by law.

3. Term of Office. Caucus members shall serve for two-year terms beginning January 1 following their election at Annual Meetings. No caucus-selected Executive Committee member may serve on the committee for more than six (6) consecutive years.

4. Meetings. The Executive Committee shall hold regular monthly meetings or as the committee deems appropriate on a date to be scheduled at the discretion of the Chair either within or outside the State of Washington and shall conduct its meetings and be subject to the same rules regarding meeting notices, manner of acting, etc. as those governing the Association Board.

5. Quorum. The presence of at least one representative from each sitting caucus shall constitute a quorum of the Executive Committee.

ARTICLE VII.

OFFICERS

1. Number. The officers of the Association shall be the Chair, Vice Chair, Secretary, and Treasurer. Such other officers and assis-

tant officers as may be deemed necessary may be elected or appointed by the Board.

2. Election and Term of Office. The officers except the Secretary of the Association shall serve for two (2) year terms beginning January 1 following the Annual Meeting.

3. Vacancies. A vacancy in any office because of death, resignation, disqualification, or otherwise shall be filled by the appropriate Caucus for the unexpired portion of the term.

4. Chair. The Chair shall be the principal executive officer of the Association and, subject to the Board and Executive Committee control, shall supervise and control all of the business and affairs of the Association. When present, the Chair shall preside over all Board and Executive Committee meetings. With the secretary or other officer of the Association authorized by the Executive Committee, the Chair may sign deeds, mortgages, bonds, contracts, or other instruments that the Board or Executive Committee has authorized to be executed, except when the signing and executing thereof has been expressly delegated by the Board, Executive Committee, or by these Bylaws to some other officer or agent of the Association or is required by law to be otherwise signed or executed by some other office or in some other manner. In general, the Chair shall perform all duties incident to the office of Chair and such other duties as may be prescribed by the Board from time to time.

The Chair shall serve one 2-year non-renewable term. The office of the Chair shall be rotated amongst the Caucuses, with a member of a particular Caucus serving as the Association Chair once every three or more terms, depending upon the number of Caucuses.

5. Vice Chair. In the absence of the Chair or in the event of the Chair's death, inability, or refusal to act, the Vice Chair shall perform the duties of the Chair, and when so acting shall have all the powers of and be subject to all the restrictions upon the Chair. The Vice Chair shall perform such other duties as from time to time

may be assigned to him or her by the Chair or by the Board or Executive Committee.

The Vice Chair shall serve one 2-year non-renewable term and shall serve as the Chair-elect. The office of the Vice Chair shall be rotated amongst the Caucuses, with a member of a particular Caucus serving as the Vice Chair once every three or more terms, depending upon the number of Caucuses.

6. Secretary. The Executive Minister shall serve as the Secretary and shall: (1) keep the minutes of the Board and Executive Committee meetings in one or more books provided for that purpose; (2) see that all notices are duly given in accordance with the provisions of these Bylaws or as required by law; (3) be custodian of the corporate records and of the seal of the Association and see that the seal of the Association is affixed to all documents, the execution of which on behalf of the Association under its seal is duly authorized; (4) keep a register of addresses of member churches and of each Board member; and (5) in general perform all duties incident to the office of secretary and such other duties as from time to time may be assigned to him or her by the Chair, Executive Committee, or by the Board.

The Executive Minister shall be elected by the Membership at a regular Annual Meeting or Special Meeting by consensus of the delegates present. Additional duties to those above should be named by a search committee formed for the purpose of determining such duties and securing a person to put in nomination before the membership. The search committee shall be comprised of no less than two representatives from each existing caucus within the Association.

7. Treasurer. The Treasurer shall have charge and custody of and be responsible for all funds and securities of the Association; receive and give receipts for moneys due and payable to the Association from any source whatsoever; and deposit all such moneys in the name of the Association in such banks, trust com-

panies, or other depositaries as shall be selected in accordance with the provisions of these Bylaws and in general perform all of the duties incident to the office of treasurer and such other duties as from time to time may be assigned to him or her by the Chair, Executive Committee, or by the Board.

The Treasurer shall serve for a 2-year term which may be renewed for one additional 2-year term. The office of the Treasurer shall be rotated amongst the Caucuses, with a member of a particular Caucus serving as the Treasurer once every six or more terms, depending upon the number of Caucuses.

8. Delegation. In the case of the absence or inability to act on the part of any officer of the Association or of any person herein authorized to act in his place, the Board may from time to time delegate the power or duties of such officer to any other officer or Executive Committee Member or Board Member or other person whom it may select.

ARTICLE VIII.
INDEMNIFICATION

To the full extent permitted by the Washington Nonprofit Corporation Act, the corporation shall indemnify any person who was or is a party to any civil, criminal, administrative, or investigative action, suit, or proceeding (whether brought by or in the right of the corporation or otherwise) by reason of the fact that he or she is or was a trustee or officer of this corporation, or is or was serving at the request of the corporation as a director, trustee or officer of another corporation, whether for profit or not for profit, against expenses (including attorney's fees), judgments, fines, and amount paid in settlement actually and reasonably incurred by him or her in connection with such action, suit, or proceeding; the Board may, at any time, approve indemnification of any other person which the corporation had the power to indemnify under the Washington Nonprofit Corporation Act.

The indemnification provided by this Article shall not be deemed exclusive of any other rights to which a person may be entitled as a matter of law or by contract. The corporation may purchase and maintain indemnification insurance for any person to the extent provided by applicable law.

ARTICLE IX.
SEAL

The seal of this Association shall consist of the name of the Association, the State of its incorporation, and the year of its incorporation.

ARTICLE X.
FISCAL YEAR

The fiscal year of the Association shall be the twelve month period beginning January 1st of each calendar year and ending the last day of December.

ARTICLE XI.
AMENDMENTS

The Delegates shall have power to make, alter, amend, and repeal the Bylaws of the Association at any Annual or special meeting of the Membership upon the affirmation of at least three-quarters of the delegates present provided such amendments are mailed or emailed to the membership two (2) weeks prior to the meeting.

ARTICLE XII.
EXEMPT ACTIVITIES

Notwithstanding any other provision of these Bylaws, no Board Member, officer, employee, or representative of this Association shall take any action or carry on any activity by or on behalf of the Association not permitted to be taken or carried on by an organization exempt under Section 501©(3) of the

Internal Revenue Code and its Regulations as they now exist or as they may hereafter be amended, or by an organization contributions to which are deductible under Section 170©(2) of such Code and Regulations as they now exist or as they may hereafter be amended.

ARTICLE XIII.
ADOPTION AND INITIAL MEETINGS

These bylaws shall be adopted by consensus at a meeting of Delegates of Churches listed as Evergreen Baptist Association Churches on February 22, 2003. An initial meeting of the delegates shall be held to select the first Executive Committee and officers who shall call the first meeting of the Association Board to begin the ministry of the Association and plan the first annual meeting in October of 2003.

ADOPTED by the Delegates of the EVERGREEN BAPTIST ASSOCIATION this 22nd day of February, 2003.

AMENDED by members of the Evergreen Association of American Baptist Churches Annual Meeting this 12th day of October 2013.

APPENDIX

CONSENSUS DEFINED

"A group reaches consensus on a decision when every member can agree to support that decision." *From How to Make Collaboration Work: Powerful Ways to Build Consensus, Solve Problems, and Make Decisions* by David Straus, published by Berret-Koehler, San Francisco, 2002, page 58.

PHASES OF CONSENSUS

David Straus's Phases of Consensus (p. 61):

Phase 1. Perception: Is there a problem? How do you feel about it? Is it legitimate to discuss the problem openly?

Phase 2. Definition: What is the problem? What are its limits or boundaries?

Phase 3. Analysis: Why does the problem exist? What are its causes?

Phase 4. Generation of Alternatives: What are some possible solutions to the problem?

Phase 5. Evaluation: What criteria must a good solution meet? Which alternatives are better or more acceptable than others?

Phase 6. Decision Making: Which solution can we agree on? Which alternative can we commit to implementing?

ANOTHER MODEL OF CONSENSUS BUILDING

1. The proposal is read to the group.

2. A few minutes (like 15) are allowed for discussion, clarification, and incorporation of concerns.

3. A straw poll is taken as a test for consensus.

4. If the straw poll indicates unanimous agreement, the proposal is passed.

5. If the straw poll is lopsided (2/3 in favor of the proposal):
   a. Proposer and others work on alternative proposals (15 minutes).
   b. Proposal is reconsidered by the group.
   c. A straw poll is taken.
      1). If a consensus is reached, the revised proposal is passed.
      2). If no consensus is reached, start over on this step or table the matter for later consideration.

6. If the straw poll is close, determine if the matter is important by a simple hand vote.
   a. If there is no clear majority on the importance of the matter, table it.
   b. If there is a clear majority (2/3) on the importance of the matter, return to #5 above.

LEVELS OF CONSENSUS

When people talk of consensus it does not necessarily mean that everyone agrees to the proposal at the same level.

1. Some may wholeheartedly agree.
2. Others may agree in principle.
3. Others may agree but have some reservations but are willing to live with the decision of the group. If everyone is in agreement at least to this level you may have consensus. If a majority of people only agree at #3, more work may be recommended to have a greater number at #1.
4. Others may agree with serious questions but will not block the group moving forward. These questions in most circumstances are best addressed in such a way that people can be more comfortable with the decision.
5. The deal breaker is when others have questions that mean they cannot support the proposal. This means that the proposal is blocked from moving forward.

APPENDIX B

American Baptist Churches USA Identity Statement 1998

"We Are American Baptists"
(revised 6/19/98)
We Are American Baptists" is an expression of Christian Faith representative of American Baptists adopted by the covenanting partners of American Baptist Churches in the U.S.A., 6/19/98. "We Are American Baptists" can be found in the Standing Rules, under Addendum #1.

American Baptists worship the triune God of the Bible, who is eternally one God in three persons. This one, true God is most clearly revealed to us in the incarnate Son, Jesus Christ our Lord.

American Baptists proclaim the Good News of the atoning death and resurrection of Jesus Christ, knowing that salvation (forgiveness of sins, release from guilt and condemnation, reconciliation with God) and eternal life are granted in grace to all who trust Jesus Christ as Savior and Lord. This Gospel is the central message of the Bible.

American Baptists believe that the Bible, composed of the Old and New Testaments, is the divinely inspired Word of God, the final written authority and trustworthy for faith and practice. It is to be interpreted responsibly under the guidance of the Holy Spirit within the community of faith. The primary purpose of the Bible is to point to Jesus Christ, the living Lord of the Church.

Although Baptists have produced numerous confessions to express our common understandings of Christian faith, we hold the Scriptures, the Old and New Testaments, as our final authority. We accept no humanly devised confession or creed as binding.

American Baptists affirm that God is sovereign over all and that this sovereignty is expressed and realized through Jesus Christ. Therefore, we affirm the Lordship of Christ over the world and the church. We joyously confess that Jesus Christ is Savior and Lord.

We are called in loyalty to Jesus Christ to proclaim the power of the Holy Spirit, the Good News of God's reconciling grace, and to declare the saving power of the Gospel to every human being and to every human institution. We celebrate Christ's charge to "make disciples of all nations" and to bear witness to God's redeeming reign in human affairs.

American Baptists are summoned to this mission in common with all Christians. With the whole body of Christ, we also believe that God has been revealed in Jesus Christ as in no other, and that "God was in Christ reconciling the world to Himself" (II Corinthians 5:18). We anticipate the day when every creature and all creation, on earth and beyond, will confess that Jesus Christ is Lord (Philippians 2:10-11).

God has given this particular community of believers called Baptists a distinctive history and experience. As we share in common with Christians everywhere, so Baptists everywhere celebrate a common heritage.

THEREFORE...With Baptist brothers and sisters around the world, we believe:

That the Bible is the final authority and trustworthy for faith and practice. It is to be interpreted responsibly under the guidance of God's Holy Spirit within the community of faith;

That the Church is a gathered fellowship of regenerated believers, a sign of the coming universal reign of God;

That the freedom to respond to the Lordship of Christ in all circumstances is fundamental to the Christian gospel and to human dignity; and

That witness to Christ is the ongoing task of every Christian and of every church.

Within the larger Baptist family, American Baptists emphasize convictions which direct our special task and ministry.

We affirm that God through Jesus Christ calls us to be:

A Redeemed People

- who claim a personal relationship to God through Jesus Christ;
- who follow the Lord in believer's baptism;
- who gather as a believer's church;
- who share in the meal of the kingdom known as the Lord's Supper;
- who honor the priesthood of all believers; and
- who live their faith as visible saints.

A Biblical People

- who affirm the centrality of Scripture in our lives;
- who pursue the study of God's inspired Word as a mandate for faith and practice; and
- who seek the guidance of the Holy Spirit for the understanding of Scripture, while respecting the common interpretation of Scripture within the community of believers.

A Worshiping People

- who gather regularly to praise God;
- who receive nourishment by communion with the Risen Christ;
- who share an open and public confession of faith; and
- who believe that personal devotion brings vitality to corporate celebration.

A Mission People

- who strive to fulfill the Great Commission to make disciples;
- who invite persons to receive salvation and follow Christ;

• who engage in educational, social, and health ministries;

• who seek justice for all persons; and

• who provide prayer and financial support to sustain a worldwide mission outreach.

An Interdependent People

• who affirm the Church's unity as given in Jesus Christ;

• who gladly embody in our practice the ministry of the whole people of God;

• who recognize God's gifts for ministry and honor all offices of pastoral ministry;

• who live and work together "in association;" and

• who bring the free church tradition to cooperative and ecumenical Christianity.

A Caring People

• who care for the needy, the weak, and the oppressed;

• who care for the earth and for all its creatures;

An Inclusive People

• who, gifted by a variety of backgrounds, find unity in diversity and diversity in unity;

• who embrace a pluralism of race, ethnicity, and gender; and

• who acknowledge that there are individual differences of conviction and theology.

A Contemporary People

• who have a remembrance for the past and a vision for the future;

• who are committed to religious liberty and to the separation of church and state; :who call our present world to make Jesus Christ Lord of all life; and

• who trust the Holy Spirit for insight and power to live in the present age.

We further believe

• That God has called us forth to such an hour as this;

- That we live with a realizable hope;
- That all things are held together in Christ;
- That all creation will find its ultimate fulfillment in God;
- That we shall see the One whose we are; and
- That Jesus shall reign for ever and ever.

APPENDIX C

ABCUSA Code of Ethics for Ministerial Leaders

Having accepted God's call to leadership in Christ's Church, I covenant with God to serve Christ and the Church, and with the help of the Holy Spirit, to deepen my obedience to the Two Great Commandments: to love the Lord our God with all my heart, soul, mind and strength, and to love my neighbor as myself.

In affirmation of this commitment, I will abide by the Code of Ethics of the Ministers Council of the American Baptist Churches and I will faithfully support its purposes and ideals. As further affirmation of my commitment, I covenant with my colleagues in ministry that we will hold one another accountable for fulfillment of all the public actions set forth in our Code of Ethics.

- I will hold in trust the traditions and practices of our American Baptist Churches; I will not accept a position in the American Baptist family unless I am in accord with those traditions and practices; nor will I use my influence to alienate my congregation/constituents or any part thereof from its relationship and support of the denomination. If my convictions change, I will resign my position.
- I will respect and recognize the variety of calls to ministry among my American Baptist colleagues and other Christians.
- I will seek to support all colleagues in ministry by building constructive relationships wherever I serve, both with the staff where I work and with colleagues in neighboring churches.

• I will advocate adequate compensation for my profession. I will help lay persons and colleagues to understand that ministerial leaders should not expect or require fees for pastoral services from constituents they serve, when these constituents are helping pay their salaries.

• I will not seek personal favors or discounts on the basis of my ministerial status.

• I will maintain a disciplined ministry in such ways as keeping hours of prayers and devotion, endeavoring to maintain wholesome family relationships, sexual integrity, financial responsibility, regularly engaging in educational and recreational activities for ministerial and personal development. I will seek to maintain good health habits.

• I will recognize my primary obligation to the church or employing group to which I have been called, and will accept added responsibilities only if they do not interfere with the overall effectiveness of my ministry.

• I will personally and publicly support my colleagues who experience discrimination on the basis of gender, race, ethnicity, age, marital status, national origin, physical impairment or disability.

• I will not proselytize from other Christian churches.

• I will, upon my resignation or retirement, sever my ministerial leadership relations with my former constituents, and will not make ministerial contacts in the field of another ministerial leader without his/her request and/or consent.

• I will hold in confidence and treat as confidential communication any information provided to me with the expectation of privacy. I will not disclose such information in private or public except when, in my practice of ministry, I am convinced that the sanctity of confidentiality is outweighed by my well-founded belief that life-threatening or substantial harm will be caused.

• I will not use my ministerial status, position or authority knowingly to abuse, misguide, negatively influence, manipulate, or take advantage of anyone, especially children.

• I will report all instances of abuse as required by law to the appropriate agency. In any case involving persons working in ABC ministry, I will also report the circumstances to the appropriate regional and/or national denominational representative.

• I will show my personal love for God as revealed in Jesus Christ in my life and ministry, as I strive together with my colleagues to preserve the dignity, maintain the discipline and promote the integrity of the vocation to which we have been called.

Notes

Chapter 2

1. Peck, M. Scott. 1987. *The Different Drum: Community Making and Peace*. New York: Simon and Schuster, pp. 73–76.
2. The name of the group honors the first African American to serve as staff on a national body in the ABC, Rev. Dr. William T. McKee, who was Executive Director of Educational Ministries.
3. Hofstede, Geert. 1980. *Culture's Consequences: International Dif-ferences in Work-Related Values*. Beverly Hills, CA: Sage Publications.
4. Hofstede, G. (2016. September 12) Country by country scores on the Hofstede Dimensions http://geert-hofstede.com/japan.html
5. Hofstede, G. (2016. September 12) Country by country scores on the Hofstede Dimensions http://geert-hofstede.com/united-states.html.
6. http://geert-hofstede.com/japan.html.
7. Ibid.
8. http://geert-hofstede.com/united-states.html.
9. Ting-Toomey, Stella. 1999. *Communicating Across Cultures*. New York: Guilford Press, pp. 103–106.
10. Hammer, Mitchell. R. *Intercultural Conflict Style Inventory: Facilitator's Manual*. Ocean Pines, MD: Hammer Consulting, LLC, p. 16. www.icsinventory.com.

Chapter 3

1. Law, Eric 1993. *The Wolf Shall Dwell with the Lamb: A Spirituality for Leadership in a Multicultural Community*. St. Louis, MO: Chalice Press.

2. Law, Eric (2016, September 13) Tools in Kaleidoscope Institute website under tools. http://www.kscopeinstitute.org/ respectful-communication-guidelines/.
3. Actually, the first time we did this we didn't have a stick, but we did have a Native American flute that we passed around our small group. In response, Bev Spears made several small "talking sticks" for us that we used in our smaller group setting.
4. Law, Eric 1993. *The Wolf Shall Dwell with the Lamb: A Spirituality for Leadership in a Multicultural Community.* St. Louis, MO: Chalis Press, pp. 115–119.

Chapter 4

1. Bennett, Milton J. 1993. *Towards a Developmental Model of Intercultural Sensitivity* and Bennett, Janet M. 1993. *Cultural Marginality: Identity Issues in Intercultural Training.* In R. Michael Paige, (ed.) *Education for the Intercultural Experience.* Yarmouth, ME: Intercultural Press. Taken from the Handout Packet for the 2010 Summer Institute for Intercultural Communication, *Training Design for Intercultural Learning.*

Chapter 5

The National Black Caucus of the American Baptist Churches USA was founded in the early 1970s to be sure that there was attention paid to having enough African American representatives on the governing board of ABCUSA and in its national staff. Rather quickly after that the National Hispanic Caucus and National Asian Caucus (now called the Alliance of Asian American Baptist Churches) were formed, and subsequently the National Indian Caucus. Eventually the National Haitian and Portuguese-speaking Caucuses were added. These were all structurally caucuses of the General Board. Since a restructure of the governance of ABCUSA in 2013, the caucuses have more than the original caucus function of being sure that there are representatives and all have embraced a ministry with, as well as for, the churches they represent.

Epilogue

1. We called Pastor Guadalupe Vasquez as a Latino church planter in 2011. After he had begun his work, he told us that while he and his family were visiting his wife's family in a village in Venezuela in 2009, he planted a church. When the church was not comfortable with associating with denominations in Venezuela, Guadalupe told them they needed to be in association with American Baptists. ABCUSA charter doesn't work that way, but Evergreen said yes. We agreed to build a relationship with Nueva Vida Commuidad Cristiana in La Aquadita and to assist them in any way we could toward building an association of churches in Venezuela that were of like mind and heart. That one church has begun planting another, and the work has begun toward building that association!